Nine Lessons
I Learned from
My Father

Murray Howe

VIKING

VIKING

an imprint of Penguin Canada, a division of Penguin Random House Canada Limited

Canada • USA • UK • Ireland • Australia • New Zealand • India • South Africa • China

First published 2017

www.penguinrandomhouse.ca

LIBRARY AND ARCHIVES CANADA CATALOGUING IN PUBLICATION

Howe, Murray (Murray A.), author
Nine lessons I learned from my father / Murray Howe.

Issued in print and electronic formats.
ISBN 978-0-7352-3417-8 (hardcover).--ISBN 978-0-7352-3418-5 (EPUB)

1. Howe, Gordie, 1928-2016. 2. Howe, Murray (Murray A.).
3. Hockey players--Canada--Biography. 4. Fathers and sons. I. Title.

GV848.5.H6H69 2017   796.962092   C2017-900167-1
                                                C2017-900452-2

Cover and interior design by Five Seventeen
Cover image: The Detroit News

Printed and bound in the United States of America

10 9 8 7 6 5 4 3 2 1

Penguin
Random House
Canada
VIKING

to my parents,
for your beautiful example

CONTENTS

INTRODUCTION

Dad passed away on June 10, 2016, exactly one year to the day after he moved in with my wife and me.

Many of us have the experience of caring for someone who once cared for us. My wife, Colleen, and I knew it wouldn't be easy. Dad was a 210-pound fall risk who'd rather die than use a walker. He prided himself on his appearance, but his eighty-seven-year-old body needed assistance with shaving, showering, dressing, and combing his wavy silver locks. His short-term memory was, as he put it, "Not worth sh*t." Not that he would ever use these words in the presence of women or children, gallant as he was, even at eighty-seven.

He would need constant reassurance and reminders of where we were and what date and time it was. This was a man who had done countless personal appearances over the past fifty years. He was always convinced that he was supposed to be getting ready for something. He just didn't quite know what.

For Colleen and me, it was an honor and a privilege to provide a home for Dad to spend the balance of his days. Both of my parents had been so good to all the Howe children and grandchildren, as well as to everyone else they met, that we were eager to repay their kindness as best we could. I'm a physician, and Coll and I both adored my dad, so my siblings knew that dad would be in good hands. I felt blessed to be able to make the most of every day, take him on outings I knew he'd enjoy, and just listen intently to the stories he was so eager to tell, even though I couldn't always understand everything he was saying. It didn't matter; the substance of the story was in his eyes, his smile, and his laughter. I understood.

I recognize that most boys are in awe of their fathers. I both feared and adored mine. Dad was scary as hell to me when I was a toddler. Grown men were afraid of him, and for good reason. Can you even imagine how big he seemed to a three-year-old who was the runt of the litter? To me, there was no measurable difference between my dad, a rhino, and an adult male silverback gorilla.

Yet I treasured him as much as any son could, because beneath his powerful exterior he was so fun-loving and gentle. He was tirelessly nurturing to me, my siblings, and my mom, and also so warm and welcoming to every person he met. The love he had for others—and his willingness to serve them—never seemed to end. There was no one I idolized more.

Like most sons, I would have loved my father no matter what he did for a living. But not every son gets to see that the rest of the world admires his dad nearly as much as he does. Nowhere was this more obvious than at Dad's second home: Detroit's Olympia Stadium. I was fortunate enough to be able to ride down to the arena with my father on occasion. He'd always arrive several hours before game time. He loved being early.

At the Olympia, he'd take the time to talk to every person he ran into, beginning with the parking lot attendant. "Hey, Gordie!" called the attendant, his face lighting up the moment he saw my dad's big grin. The attendants always offered to park Dad's car, and he always declined. He would rather carry his car than have someone else park it for him. He hated having anyone do anything for him. If a hotel porter tried to grab his suitcase from him, the poor fellow would receive a solid elbow to the ribs. Dad would carry his own bags but tip the porter anyway.

We typically entered the Olympia through the main door, avoiding the secret back entrance where players could duck the crowd. The police officers working the game were among the first to greet him. "Hey, Mr. Hockey! How's that elbow?" they would joke.

"I dunno. You tell me!" was my dad's usual response. Then he would graze past them, dragging his elbow across their faces as he went. Who else could get away with that?

I'd follow in Dad's huge wake, and Detroit's finest would give me a wink or a thumbs-up. All the Howe kids were so well known at the stadium that we breezed right past the police and the ticket takers.

Once we were inside the arena, everyone was so excited to be around him, it was electrifying. That charged my father right up.

The hot dog lady would say, "Gordie, how about a dog? Or a Coke?"

Dad would chuckle, "Maybe after the game!"

Fans recognized him instantly. There'd be an endless stream of "Hey, Gordie!" or "Here comes Mr. Elbows!"

Dad always acted like it was the first time he'd ever heard that one.

Once he'd made it to the dressing room, he'd slowly undress, painstakingly folding or hanging each article of clothing and placing his shoes in perfect parallel in their little cubby. He'd then take forever to don his equipment, retape his stick, and sharpen his skates if they weren't exactly to his liking.

Even if I had never seen him step out onto the ice, he would be a legend in my eyes. He's who I wanted to be. I still pinch myself at the realization that he was my father. How many sons are genuinely excited to ask their fathers for an autograph? The older I got, the more my awe and admiration for him grew. He was as huge as I am compact. As legendary as I am ordinary. Perhaps the only things I inherited from him were his nose and his sense of humor. Yet I always considered myself blessed beyond measure.

I remember those python-sized arms scooping me up from the back seat of our car in the wee hours of the night after a game and delivering me delicately into my bed when I was about six years old. I remember faking sleep because I wanted him to carry me. The same juggernaut who had just dazzled thousands of fans with his ferocious power and grace was the one gently tucking me into bed.

———

And then the giant who used to tuck me in was gone forever. It was hard to believe my dad had really passed away. He had seemed immortal. Indestructible. I'd seen him come back from so many injuries and near-death experiences, it hardly seemed real this time. The day he died, after his body was transported to the funeral home, I kept expecting him to walk right through the front door with a big smile and shout, "Just kidding!"

Only a few weeks earlier, he had made back-to-back appearances to kick off the Gordie Howe Initiative for traumatic brain injury in Toledo, Ohio. He wowed the hundreds of attendees, posed for photographs, elbowed the guys, and hugged the gals.

A few days after that event, however, Dad lost his appetite and developed a fulminant pneumonia with a deep cough, a high fever, low blood pressure, and severely labored breathing. He appeared septic. I slept alongside him all night, thinking that it could be his last. I thought about bringing him to the emergency room. But my thirty years of experience as a physician convinced me that he would be admitted, then spiral downhill in a cold, sterile ICU. I pictured him in a state of limbo—intubated, sedated, but still unable to rest because of the incessant hissing of the ventilator and the frightening tangle of EKG leads, chest tubes, nasogastric tubes, IV lines, arterial lines, central venous catheters, and restraints tethering him to the bed. The endless cavalcade of masked strangers in scrubs and white uniforms would hardly add comfort. I had seen such scenarios play out too many times. I did not want him to die like that. Nor did he.

I called my family and informed them that I thought Dad was preparing for liftoff, and that they should come right away to say their goodbyes. I arranged for a hospice nurse to determine whether he was a candidate for end-of-life care. The following day the nurse stopped by, and in short order she determined that my dad was actively dying. He had a few days—perhaps a week—to live, she told me. The family should plan accordingly.

I called each of my siblings and reiterated what the hospice nurse had said. I also decided to treat Mr. Hockey with a Z-Pak oral antibiotic to see if it would help, although I was doubtful given his condition.

My brother Mark was on the earliest flight he could arrange. My sister, Cathy, texted me from her car in Lubbock, Texas, with her daughter, Jaime, and grandson Brenden, and said, "We're driving. We'll be there as soon as we can." My brother Marty called and said he'd be in shortly with his wife, Mary. My daughter, Meaghan, headed down from Detroit with her husband, Doug, and her sister-in-law, Jen Raine. Mark's daughter, Azia, and his granddaughters Ella and Lahna also mobilized, as did his sons, Nolan and Travis; their spouses, Christine and Kristine; and Travis's daughter, Ainsley.

We scrambled to make room for everyone at our home. My wife, Colleen, keen on logistics, was skeptical that we could reasonably host my entire family, as well as Dad, his caregivers, the hospice nurses, and any friends, neighbors, and fans who wished to stop by. We decided to wing it.

Everyone was dealing with a range of emotions, from grief to guilt to angst and anxiety, as well as grappling with the prospect of their own mortality. At the same time, there were a lot of tough decisions to be made: What medicines do we discontinue? Which hospice medicines do we use, and how often? What foods and fluids do we offer? Is he better off in his bed or sitting upright in a chair? Even with a medical degree, I found all these decisions challenging, so it's no wonder that it was nearly impossible for our family to arrive at a consensus on anything. I decided the best approach was to chill. Nothing explodes at zero degrees kelvin. Whenever it got heated, I went out for a run or took my nephew Brenden for a hike in the woods. That's what Dad would do.

Meanwhile, my father rallied. His breathing slowed and became more regular, and his blood pressure normalized. The hospice nurse returned twenty-four hours after the initial visit. "Hmmm, he doesn't look so bad now," she remarked.

Mr. Hockey was sleeping comfortably and his fever was gone. He seemed to be smiling in his slumber. By the time all the family had arrived, he was unmistakably smiling, alert, and able to converse. He sure didn't look like he was dying. We all breathed a sigh of relief. We've still got some more time with him, I thought. Just in case, we arranged for a chaplain to hold a prayer service while the entire family was still in town. We surrounded Mr. Hockey, propping his head up on his Red Wings pillow, and prayed. He loved it and quietly, earnestly whispered in the chaplain's ear. Although we couldn't hear what he said, the weight of his gesture was profound.

But he was very weak, and he hadn't eaten or drunk much in the past few days. Standing and walking were becoming difficult without assistance. So he mostly lounged in his comfy blue recliner while everyone doted on him, vying for position at his side to offer him applesauce, ice cream, or a smoothie. He enjoyed the attention, especially from his granddaughters, and appeared to get a little stronger every day. Each time the hospice nurse visited, she said, "Hmmm, he seems a little better than the last time I saw him." He appeared to have no pain, no anxiety, no distress; he was completely at peace. If he was dying, he was doing it gracefully, just as he did everything else.

After a week of love and affection, Mr. Hockey appeared to have no intention of dying anytime soon. The family decided that they would return home. I was to call everyone if Dad took another downturn.

But as soon as everyone left, something was different about Dad. For the first time in his life, he had no interest in food. The bodyguards (we affectionately referred to his caregivers as "bodyguards" because Dad didn't want anyone taking care of him) knew all his favorite snacks, and offered him doughnuts, cookies, and ice cream, but he wouldn't take the bait. Not even a nibble. At most, he allowed us to wet his whistle with a few sips of chocolate milk or orange juice.

It seemed as if he had made a decision that if he couldn't go for walks, visit the hockey rink, push the grocery cart, hug the ladies, or tease the little kids, he was no longer having fun. And it was time to do something else. Without sustenance he rapidly grew weaker and less alert, but he remained in no distress. I called my siblings again, and suggested that they come back, because this time it seemed to be for real. I slept with Dad again that night, thinking it might be his last. But he was still alive the next morning, after twenty-four hours with nothing by mouth. Same with the next night. And the next. And the next. And the next. As family returned, we took turns holding his hand and lying down with him. We didn't want him to be alone.

Although Dad was dying, the mood within our home evolved from apprehension to peace. Dad's calm demeanor spread through the household. Each of us took turns telling him how we felt about him and sharing our favorite memories. I can easily summarize the substance of these conversations in a few words: "I love you, Dad. Thank you for being the best dad ever. God is waiting for you. You can go whenever you are ready. We will be fine."

He lasted seven days with no food or water, yet he was peaceful throughout. There was no pain and no fear—just a resolve to move on. On the day before he died, his former lineman-turned-bodyguard Lionel and I rolled him in a wheelchair out to the patio by the pool. It was a gorgeous sunny day. He hated wheelchairs and would sit in one only under the direst of circumstances. This was pretty dire. A few of his most devoted friends and neighbors sat with him, taking in the warmth and splendor. Howes of different generations gathered. Dad's other caregivers, John and Pedro, stayed to keep Mr. Hockey company, even though they were off the clock. They had become loyal friends as well as fans. Although Mr. Hockey didn't open his eyes, he clearly enjoyed the serenity. One last time to savor the outdoors.

After I rolled him back inside early that afternoon, Dad's breathing pattern changed. Each breath was more rapid and deep. The hospice nurse said it was a matter of minutes to hours at that point. But that night, surrounded by family, Dad was still with us. By 1:00 a.m., everyone had drifted off to sleep except Meaghan, Mark, and me. I finally conked out next to Dad on the couch while still resting my hand on his huge forearm. Meaghan eventually retired from the same couch in search of a bed. Mark also went to bed at some point, but then he awoke at about 5:00 a.m. and came back to continue the vigil.

I was startled awake at 7:57 a.m. I felt like Mr. Hockey's spirit literally tapped me on the shoulder and said, "See ya, Muzz! You be good!" I bolted upright, looked at Dad, and then turned to Mark, who said, "I think he's gone."

I looked again at Dad. He took one more deep breath and let it out slowly. And that was his last.

———

By 8:30 a.m., a television news crew was at our door asking if Mr. Hockey had passed away. I was totally caught off guard. I was on my way to open the door in my pajamas, thinking it was a neighbor dropping off some breakfast (our neighbors had generously adopted our entire family for the week, dropping off enough food each day to feed twenty hungry Howes). Fortunately, Pedro got to the door first. He assessed the situation and told the film crew to get lost. Mr. and Mrs. Hockey had always taught us to be respectful of the media, but in this circumstance, I gave Pedro two thumbs-up.

By 9:00 a.m., the news appeared to have gone global, despite Pedro's efforts, and despite the fact that Dad had yet to be officially pronounced dead. We instructed the funeral director to pick up Mr. Hockey's body in an unmarked vehicle and drive to the back of our home to avoid the TV cameras. Once he'd arrived, we rolled Dad out the back door, guided him into the back of a station wagon, and said our goodbyes.

And then he was gone.

Immediately I sensed a gaping chasm in our kitchen and breakfast nook. Dad had taken up so much space, both literally and figuratively, that without him the room felt the size of a high school gymnasium. Every area where he'd spent time in the past year suddenly seemed vast and cold. His bedroom. The family room. The patio. The basement, including the room where we had played tennis-ball hockey for two decades. He had left an immeasurable void.

The moment they heard of Dad's passing, the Red Wings staff, representing the Ilitch family, contacted us and offered up Joe Louis Arena as a site for a public viewing. They said they would handle all the details. This is only one small example of what makes the Ilitch family such a rare treasure.

All day, the phone rang off the hook with people calling to offer condolences and share their favorite memories of Dad. The house filled up with relatives and friends as well, and soon the kitchen was jammed with people making coffee or warming up donated meals. Amid the chaos, it suddenly dawned on me that I still had a eulogy to prepare. My family had agreed at a meeting some years ago that I would be the one to pay tribute to Dad. I was thrilled and deeply honored. What a privilege to eulogize my father—my hero.

I bid the troops farewell and retreated to my bedroom, closed the door, and knelt alongside my bed as if to pray. But instead, I opened my computer on the bedspread. I spent the next nine hours grappling with the emptiness that had filled the house. Eventually I watched the sun rise. Sure I was tired, but I was also gratified: out of my persistence, my dad—the magnificent, one-of-a-kind man and father—had begun to emerge.

Most of my childhood was dedicated to trying to be just like my dad, Gordie Howe, the indomitable hockey player. Only later did I come to realize that who I really wanted to be was Gordie Howe the loving father, the thoughtful husband, and the selfless, patient, positive, generous friend to all. It would require a team of horses to stop me from sharing my reverence for this man with the rest of the world.

As I thought about Dad, it was clear to me that for him, actions most often spoke louder than words. He was raised to speak softly but carry a big stick. Usually a Northland. Thus, in order to know Gordie Howe the man, you would have to know what he *did*. This was the shape my portrait of Dad would take.

—

I thought I was done with Dad's tribute that Saturday morning, but I wasn't. When our family met with the priest on Monday, more priceless anecdotes and insights emerged from my siblings, my nieces and nephews, and my own children. Even more incredible stories came from the thousands of fans I met at the public viewing at Joe Louis Arena on Tuesday. So on Tuesday night, after getting home from Detroit well after midnight, hoarse from talking with Gordie Howe fans for over thirteen hours and now only a sunrise away from giving the eulogy, I again hammered away at my laptop until I felt the tribute was perfect. I was determined not to let Dad down.

—

Like most young boys growing up in early sixties Detroit, I dreamt of someday becoming a professional hockey player, just like my dad. It seemed almost a birthright. A *given*. Not only was Dad a pro, but so were two of my uncles, Vic and Vern. And my brothers, Marty and Mark? Well, they had scouts eyeing them before they'd finished grade school. I was obviously next in line.

I was willing to do anything and everything to be in the NHL like my dad. Frankly, I didn't consider any other path. Our entire house was a hockey shrine. The family room table had at its center a huge Red Wings logo that Mom had painstakingly fashioned out of red and white tiles. The walls were adorned with paintings and photographs of Dad in uniform. His trophies rested majestically on ledges above the fireplace mantel. Midget-sized hockey sticks were propped next to the fireplace, ready for the next round of "carpet hockey" using a balled-up sock, a tape ball, a tennis ball, or, for extra excitement, a Superball. God help those trophies looming above! Our living room was adorned with coffee-table books on hockey. My bedroom shelves were filled with hockey books, Red Wings programs, and trophies, patches, and pins from various tournaments.

Our driveway saw more games than *Hockey Night in Canada*, as evidenced by the puck-pocked garage door. Much of our gear, including goalie pads, steel nets, and sticks, had been pilfered from Olympia Stadium—unwittingly donated by the likes of Sawchuk, Ullman, Oliver, Delvecchio, Mahovlich, Unger, and Redmond. I'm sure players wondered, "Where the heck is my stick? It was *right here yesterday.*" Well, Mr. Berenson, it's in Gordie Howe's garage, that's where.

When we weren't playing hockey in the driveway or family room, we were playing it on our frozen rink. As soon as I could walk, my dad put skates on me. Handed me a chair. And pointed down the ice. "Go," he said. That was Mr. Hockey's advice on Howe to skate.

I went. By the time I was four, I could skate as comfortably as I could run. I still had training wheels on my bike, but skating? No problem.

I'll spare you the details of my ill-fated odyssey to become a pro hockey player over the ensuing sixteen years, but suffice it to say, I failed miserably. Though I had all the right genes, all the right training, all the right passion, and even a Gordie Howe hockey stick, I just wasn't meant to follow in my father's skate strides.

At the age of fifteen, I played on a Junior B team with Wayne Gretzky and Paul Coffey. They later went on to rewrite the NHL's record books. I, on the other hand, distinguished myself by being selected *last* in the 1977 Ontario Hockey Association draft. Player number 228, twentieth round, by the Windsor Spitfires. Windsor will always hold a special place in my heart for having had faith in me.

The following year, I was unceremoniously axed from the University of Michigan Wolverines. It was the best thing that ever happened to me. The shock jolted me to a profound real-ization: I didn't need to be a professional hockey player to be like my father. The way for me to be like Gordie Howe wasn't by scoring goals but rather to use my talents to be the best person I could be.

That realization freed me to devote the energy and effort that I'd once channeled into hockey toward other things. Hard work, certainly. Not just doggedness, not just a willingness to submit to drudgery. I mean the joy of hard work, the ache that comes from pushing yourself and taking satisfaction in the fruits of your labor. That is, the joy of hard work that I had always seen in my father. It freed me to devote more of myself to others as well. That joy in the happiness of loved ones and strangers alike, which I had always seen in Dad. His humility, and loyalty, and generosity.

Looking back, I am struck by the irony that I became a little more like the person I admired most in the world the day I gave up on the sport I had always thought defined him, that every-one thought defined him. Dad's name was literally synonymous with hockey, but he was more than hockey. Bobby Orr and Wayne Gretzky would say pretty much the same thing: Dad was the best player in the world, but he was an even better person. So I guess when I walked out of the rink at U of M after that final practice, I wasn't giving up on hockey so much as I was setting my sights on something higher.

As I sit down to write this, I realize I have been observing my father for my whole life. I've watched him bring a crowd to its feet with athletic feats the likes of which might never be seen again, and I've seen him too frail to walk. I've seen him stare down thugs and brawlers, and I've seen his incredible acts of tenderness and generosity. I have witnessed his superhuman strength and also his moments of greatest vulnerability. I've known his love, and observed his vengeance. I've been tucked in by him, and tucked him in. After all these years, I still want to be like him. I still intend to.

Perhaps that's the greatest legacy a father can leave—that his son goes on aspiring to be like him, even after he is gone.

The lessons he taught me—through his words, of course, but more through his actions, his trials and triumphs, and his impact on others—continue to inspire me, fueling my passion for life, mankind, and the Good Lord. My hope for this book is that my father's wisdom and gentle spirit move readers to be the best they can be—to live courageously, welcome all, serve all, and treasure this precious gift we call life.

1

Live Honorably

"People depend upon you to do the right thing."

It's almost midnight on Friday night, June 10, the day my father drew his last breath. I'm kneeling at the edge of my bed, ready to tackle Dad's tribute. I'm crushed by the thought that I will never again hear his soft voice, see his impish grin, or feel his viselike "good-morning" embrace. I feel a gaping hole in my heart. It seems unimaginable to live in a world without Gordie Howe. Where do I even begin?

But I soldier on, because Dad always insisted that we kids count our blessings in the face of adversity, and never waste a second feeling sorry for ourselves. I found it easy to count my blessings because I recognized how fortunate I was to have had such giving parents. I'm eager to share my love and respect for my dad with the rest of the world. Today marks the end of an exhilarating, unforgettable roller-coaster ride. Although heart-wrenching, it was hands down the best year and a half of my life.

Each day as soon as I got home from work, Mr. Hockey and I, along with one of his caregivers, would head out to do something fun. I soon discovered that what Dad loved to do most was to *be* Mr. Hockey. To pose for pictures with fans at the local ice rink, zoo, library, mall, and grocery store. To head-lock, face-wash, or elbow the kids. Or just chase them around. And show them how to hold a hockey stick. And how to stab an opponent in the guts with it.

"He's just kidding," the dads would reassure their youngsters. Don't bet on it, I thought to myself.

So many great memories of the past year flooded over me as I stared at my laptop. I thought long and hard about this one-of-a-kind man I called Father. Obviously he was larger than life to hockey fans and friends. But he was even bigger than that to me, his son, the one he called "the little guy," even when I was fifty-five. I idolized him for all that he was, and did my best to follow his lead. But although he was a man of strong conviction, he spoke softly and judiciously, and taught mostly by example.

Staring at the screen, I asked myself, What did I learn from my father? What did he stand for? My first thought, without hesitation, was *live honorably.*

HONORABLE: honest, moral, ethical, principled,
    righteous, right-minded; decent, respectable,
    estimable, virtuous, good, upstanding, upright,
    worthy, noble, fair, just, truthful, trustworthy, reliable,
    reputable, creditable, dependable, law-abiding.*

---

* *Oxford American Writer's Thesaurus,* 3rd ed. (New York: Oxford University Press, 2012), p. 429.

Yep, that was Dad. A man who stood up anytime a woman entered the room. Even when he was eighty-eight years old.

Mr. Hockey stood for nothing if not for honor. Honor through loyalty, respect for self and for others, and excellence in every endeavor.

Lorne Richardson, a teammate of my father's from King George School in Saskatoon, shared with me his account of Mr. Hockey's gallantry. In 1946, seventeen Saskatoon boys travelled to Detroit for a tryout with the Red Wings. Upon the players' arrival at the Olympia, Jack Adams, the legendary Red Wings coach, informed them that he had some bad news: there were not enough rooms to house them all, so some would have to volunteer to sleep under the bleachers at the stadium on makeshift cots. Dad was the youngest player there but the first to volunteer.

Lorne approached him later and praised him for volunteering. Dad said, "Oh hell, I wasn't trying to be nice. I just figure I'll be able to stay on the ice after everybody leaves!" The following morning they were up early for tryouts. Lorne asked my dad how he slept. "Not very well," he replied. "There were rats the size of coyotes running over our beds!"

But it's what happened next that Lorne remembers most of all. There were two groups assigned to try out. The A group would skate for an hour, followed by the B group. Dad was in the A group, but when their time was up and the B group took the ice, Mr. Hockey just stayed out there for another hour. He later told Lorne that he just wanted to make sure the Wings noticed him. Lorne recalled, "Even though your dad was the youngest, he led by example. His hard work and humility made us all work harder."

My brother Mark once told me a story of an NHLer who played against Mr. Hockey in his last season in Hartford, in 1980. Dad unintentionally cut the young player while in a scrum for the puck in the corner. It was a nasty cut that required quite a few stitches. When the buzzer signaled the end of the period, Dad walked over to the visiting medical room and spent several minutes talking with his opponent and apologizing to him. The player later told Mark that he had never forgotten that moment and what an impression it made on him. Dad played the game according to a code of honor.

That didn't make him a pushover, though. Dad flattened opponents like a freight train, and he considered running a guy over something of a calling card. Or as he put it, "A healthy body check will be remembered." He hit opponents with such force that they frequently headed to the bench to assess their injuries—if they were able to get up at all. But he was the furthest thing from a bully on the ice. If your head was down, he would give you a heads-up before cleaning your clock. (Unless you had given him a cheap shot, that is. Even honor codes have their limits.)

Another part of his honor code was not to showboat. If he scored, he was hesitant to even raise his stick in celebration. In his eyes, every goal was a team effort. So instead of "pirouettes around the rink for the cameras," as he put it, he'd congratulate his teammates with a pat on the behind for setting up the play. I remember watching him score, hands barely raised, and only the faintest grin, and I can still feel the surge of pride that welled up in my chest; like him, I celebrated within. I've felt that same feeling many times since, any time one of my children accomplishes something grand. I'm much more excited for their successes than I am for my own. Even at yearly father–son games when I was growing up, Dad would resist the temptation to score. He played on the *kids'* team, just to even the odds a bit. He would pretty much knock down all the dads like a bull in a china shop, but instead of finishing off with a goal, he'd loft a nice saucer pass over to one of us kids right in front of the net, with a helpless dad-goalie sprawled across the crease like a walrus on an ice floe.

Naturally, the kids always won. Mr. Hockey kept the game close but made sure the sons came through in the end. And he *never* scored a goal himself. We always felt a little guilty about beating the dads. But not too much. Most of them were thrilled to have been mauled by Gordie Howe anyway.

Mr. Hockey's honor code even extended to fighting. He never started a fight—but he could be counted upon to end one. He would also lay down his life for his teammates or his coaches. When Dad was seventeen, the Wings decided to send him to Omaha, Nebraska, to their United States Hockey League (USHL) farm team. Mr. Hockey was very fortunate because Omaha had one of the finest hockey coaches of all time (in Dad's view), Tommy Ivan. Unfortunately, Ivan had many older, more experienced players, and he didn't have much confidence in my dad's ability to handle himself against these seasoned players, so he sat him on the bench for the first few months of the season.

But then came a game in which an enforcer on the other team was literally chasing one of Omaha's smaller players around the rink. Mr. Hockey couldn't take being a spectator any longer. He leapt onto the ice and beat the tar out of the tough guy. The referee had to pry him off his shell-shocked adversary. Nowadays, leaving the bench to jump into a fight will get you suspended. But not back then in Omaha. The fans loved it, and this shy but scrappy kid from Saskatchewan had just made a name for himself.

People back home already knew that bullies weren't safe from Gordie Howe. In grade five, Dad encountered a scuffle as he exited the building after the final bell. A bully who was about three years older than my dad was beating the stuffing out of a kid who was in my father's class. Dad needed to hurry home to do some work for his father, and he didn't want to be late or he knew he'd be in a heap of trouble. But he couldn't *not help*.

So he took on the bully and landed several Gordie Howitzers before the principal, Mr. Trickey, finally broke up the fight. He dragged both my dad and the bully down to the office for a "chat." Back then, a "chat" might include a hickory rod as thick as your thumb (the "rule of thumb") across your backside.

Mr. Trickey listened to each one's story, and then asked my father to wait in the hallway. From that vantage point, Dad could hear a major arse-whipping (literally), then saw the bully limp out of the office, beet red, with tears streaming down his face. Mr. Trickey handed him a piece of paper with a three-day suspension on it and sent him on his way. Then the principal looked at my dad and growled, "In my office, now!"

Once the door to Mr. Trickey's office closed, he stared at my dad for a long time, then allowed the smallest hint of a grin to escape. He looked Dad straight in the eye and said, "Gordon, do not *ever* tell anyone I said this, but I am very proud of you for standing up for the other boy. And I'm really glad you clobbered that bully. He had it coming."

Dad promised he would never tell a soul, but of course he broke that promise when he told me. By then, seventy years had passed, so I'm sure the statute of limitations for Canadian school secrets had lapsed.

When my father got home that day, he expected a whooping from his own dad for being late, but when he told Ab about the fight, Grandpa Howe just smiled at him and said, "Attaboy!" Compliments from Ab were scarce. Dad cherished that one.

———

Though Dad fought a lot in his early years, he made every effort not to permanently injure an opponent. He was a master of controlled mayhem. During a game in his last year with the Houston Aeros, in the 1976–77 season, he took a face-off and his overenthusiastic rookie opponent slashed him across his perpetually swollen, throbbing wrists. Mr. Hockey felt that the slash was not very gentlemanly, so he parked the tip of his stick blade an inch shy of his opponent's nose. The rookie backpedaled, tripping over his own skates and falling onto his behind. The crowd gasped.

The ref gave the rookie two minutes for slashing and awarded Dad a five-minute major penalty for high-sticking with intent to enucleate. After the game I told my dad that his high-stick looked really bad, like he was aiming to poke out an eye. Dad just grinned. "Awwwwwww," he said. "I wasn't gonna hurt him. I just wanted to *scare him a little.*"

Despite his ferocious nature on the ice, Dad went out of his way not to hurt his opponents. He routinely shielded the opposing goalie's face if the netminder went down in front of him. Even if it meant sacrificing a goal. Johnny Bower, the legendary Leafs goalie and Dad's fishing buddy from

Saskatchewan, could attest to that. Dad knew there'd be plenty of other opportunities to score.

Mr. Hockey's honorable ways weren't limited to the ice. He was the most loyal man I've ever known.

He never criticized his teammates, his coaches, the owner, his opponents—or anyone else, for that matter. Dad lived by the adage "If you don't have anything nice to say, don't say anything at all." He was the king of restraint.

I especially marveled at how honorably Dad treated my mom. He always held the door open for her, helped her with her coat, stood until she was seated, and never once did I hear him criticize her.

He was fiercely loyal to my mom, and referred to her as his "bride," even after more than fifty years of marriage. That didn't mean they never fought, of course. One time, in the early sixties, Mom was angry at Dad about something, and out of frustration he walked out and hopped into his car to go for a drive. My then eight-year-old brother, Mark, who hero-worshipped Dad as much as I did, jumped into the car to support him and said, "I can't believe Mom was talking bad to you!"

Dad looked him straight in the eye and said, "Don't you ever talk about your mother like that!"

Not only was Dad a model of loyalty, but he also cultivated loyalty among his teammates. They were all better because of him. They wouldn't dare disparage their wives, girlfriends, coaches, or teammates in Dad's presence. Mom and Dad set a great example of a loving, respectful, committed couple for the younger Red Wings. This was indispensible in a professional sport where husbands are on the road much of year, and are hounded by adoring groupies.

My parents established a welcoming, wholesome environment for all the new players and their significant others, setting the tone with a backyard barbeque each year. This inspired the players to bond with their wives as well as with their teammates. Especially their big right-winger. How cool was it that one of the team's most beloved stars was the one who made the effort to help the rookies feel welcome? In Dad's book, there was no room for stars—just buddies looking out for one another.

Although Dad played tough, and wanted to win more than anything, he always kept his cool. He felt a responsibility to conduct himself with class every shift. That meant never smacking his stick against the glass, cursing out an opponent, or slamming the gate shut. "What good did that do anyway?" Dad thought. Whatever anger or frustration he might have felt toward an adversary, he kept it well hidden beneath his cool exterior. At least until his opponent woke up on the bench with a headache, wondering what had just happened.

A part of being honorable is possessing uncommon courage. Mr. Hockey seemingly feared nothing. When I was about eleven, my dad and I were in New York City, standing in front of Madison Square Garden after a game. He was talking with another player when a man stepped out of the shadows, inserted himself between the two players, and said, "Hey, man, I just got outta prison, and I need some money. You got any?"

My dad said, "Excuse me, sir, but I'm having a conversation with this gentleman, and you just interrupted us. I am happy to help you out in a moment."

The guy pulled out a long knife from underneath his jacket and shot back, "I don't think you *heard me*, man. I said *give me some money.*"

The other player started backing away, as did I, but Dad didn't flinch.

"I'll tell you what"—Mr. Hockey looked him straight in the eye and began rolling up his coat sleeves, revealing two Popeye-sized forearms terminating in sledgehammer-sized fists—"if you don't walk away right now, I'm going to give you something you *didn't* ask for."

I was afraid that I was about to see my dad get stabbed to death on a cold New York street. But the mugger's eyes widened as he sized up Dad's guns, and he started backing up. He managed a threat: "Hey, man, I'll cut you!" But he didn't sounds very convincing in retreat.

Dad started walking *toward* his aggressor, who decided he'd had enough and took off running, much to my relief. I was surprised my dad didn't chase after him. If I hadn't been there, I'm sure he would have.

———

Dad cleaned up not only the streets but also every household or facility he happened upon. He loved doing the dishes, cleaning the kitchen, vacuuming, making beds—you name it. You could bounce a coin off the beds after he made them. Military corners, and never a wrinkle in the sheets or bedspread. If the kitchen sink wasn't sparkling, he'd find an old toothbrush and some Comet cleanser and go to town.

Not in a million years would he allow a stitch of clothing to remain on the floor. He'd fold it, smooth it out, and then hang it up, or rest it over the back of a chair if he was going to wear it later that day. His teaching style was very effective.

Instead of badgering us to clean up after ourselves, he'd just do it, humming all the while. Imagine the embarrassment of your hero picking up after you, especially when you're an adult!

Mr. Hockey always tried to be good. But he also took it upon himself to pass that goodness—that sense of responsibility to do the right thing—to everyone he met, especially kids. One time, I remember a young autograph-seeker thrusting a picture at him and saying, "Sign this!" Dad wrote "THIS" on the picture. I thought that was pretty funny; the boy didn't.

"Hey, you didn't sign your name!" he complained.

Mr. Hockey, feigning ignorance, explained, "But you said sign *this*."

This jousting went on for a bit before my dad finally told him, "If you'd like someone to do something for you, you need to use good manners. Then they'll be happy to help. Now what do you say?"

"Please will you sign my goddam picture, Mr. Howe," the boy said.

Actually that's not what he said, but that's how Dad liked to tell the story. In truth the young man asked politely, and Dad obliged.

Dad never hesitated to teach good manners. Many years ago, he was at one of my games at the old, dumpy Detroit Skating Club. A large ashtray had fallen over, spilling its contents, and Dave Shrader, the brother of one of my teammates, was standing right next to it.

Dad looked at Dave and said, "Please go find a broom and let's sweep that up."

"I didn't knock it over!" Dave protested.

My dad persisted. "That's not what I asked you. Now, please go get a broom."

Dave was about fourteen, very quick and very obstinate, in the manner of most fourteen-year-olds. He bolted.

Mr. Hockey gave chase. He wasn't a fast runner, but he had tenacity. He chased Dave around the parking lot until he had him cornered, then lifted him up by the scruff of his jacket like a puppy, *carried* him back inside, and plopped him down in front of the fallen ashtray.

"Now, what did I say?" Dad inquired, laughing under his breath.

David tried to stifle his smirk. He knew he had just been bested by the best. Even a rebellious teen could respect that. "Go get a broom and sweep this up," Dave replied, and then he went off to complete his mission. He knew my dad would follow him home if he didn't comply.

Not even his teammates were immune to Mr. Hockey's lessons. Our longtime family friend Felix Gatt was an eye-witness to that. Felix was a die-hard Red Wings fan as a youngster, and he waited outside the dressing room after every game, trying to get autographs. His Wings program had been signed by every player except famed netminder Terry Sawchuk.

Dad often described Terry as "Hands down one of the finest goalies anywhere." But if the Wings lost, which wasn't often in those days, Terry got moody and was hell-bent to get out of the arena. After one of those games, ten-year-old Felix saw him leaving and rushed over, explaining how important it was that he have Terry's signature to complete his collection. Sawchuk just kept walking.

Dad overheard Felix's pitch and blocked Terry's exit. He said with a chuckle, "How about signing this young man's book, Terry? If you don't, I might have to take my stick and cut you a new five hole." I'm sure Terry knew Dad was only kidding, but I suspect his respect for Dad trumped all else. Mr. Sawchuk signed the program.

Dad was staunchly dedicated to his fans. He made it a top priority to be prepared for fans at all times. He never went anywhere without a pen, and in his later years, he carried a stack of pre-signed player cards, which he knew fans would enjoy more than a signed napkin or gum wrapper. He practiced his magic tricks regularly and made sure he always had a dime that he could make "disappear" by rubbing it into his oversized elbow.

In Mr. Hockey's last years of life, when his short-term memory was failing, I was concerned that Dad might lose his penchant for excellence, manners, chivalry, and his standards for cleanliness. But that didn't happen. If he saw a piece of trash on the floor or ground anywhere, he'd pick it up. When he was too tired or stiff, he'd point to it and refuse to move until I picked it up.

Dad's graciousness was boundless. At dinner, he wouldn't eat until everyone else had started. He'd also offer his food to everyone around him before he had a bite. That was true even of the last meal of his life, a bowl of applesauce. He held the door open for men as well as women, and he refused to walk through until all women had passed—even at his last appearance, a month before he passed away. The last words he ever spoke, a few days before his death, were "Thank you."

2

Live Generously

"What good is money except to do something nice for someone?"

It's nearing 2:00 a.m. Colleen, buried in a mountain of pillows beside me, conked out almost an hour ago. Whether she's asleep or awake, I love having her close to me; there is nowhere else I'd rather be. She inspires me to soldier on.

I return to thoughts of Mr. Hockey. A man of honor, yes. But so much more. I realize tonight how extraordinarily much *more*. When I was a toddler, I just assumed all dads were really huge and played hockey for a living. Most of the dads I knew were Red Wings. It didn't occur to me that mine was no ordinary father until my third grade teacher handed out the current issue of *My Weekly Reader* and there was an article featuring Dad. My teacher and classmates were almost as surprised as I was! As I work on the eulogy, I can see more clearly than ever that the small things I saw every day taught me more than I could have imagined. I'm missing Dad terribly at the moment, but I feel an overwhelming sense of gratitude.

Whenever we went out to eat with friends, Dad always grabbed the check—unless a fan or another guest hijacked it first. And he usually wasn't content to stop there. Mom and Dad both loved to look around the restaurant for random people or families and pick up their tab anonymously. This brought them sheer joy. They would wait around to see the recipients' faces when the server informed them that their bill had been paid. It was a wonderful lesson for me on the joy in giving.

One afternoon, when Dad was visiting the Baskin Robbins where my brother Marty worked, an entire baseball team streamed in. Not only did he sign every uniform, but he also treated the whole dugout to ice cream. Dad left with more than just ice cream that day. He left a priceless impression on every one of those young men. And that's how generosity works. You always come away with more than you give.

If it weren't for that kind of generosity, there might never have been a Mr. Hockey. Back in the Depression, when my grandma Katherine (Katy) was a young mother, a neighbor appeared at the Howe doorstep. Her husband was ill and unable to work, and the woman had no money for milk for her infant. No one had much—certainly not the Howes—but this poor soul had even less. Still, she didn't want to beg. She was carrying a burlap bag filled with whatever her family could spare. She was offering it all for sale. For whatever Grandma could spare.

My grandmother scrounged together all the money she had, which was a buck fifty, plus a bag full of food. The woman was eternally grateful and handed over the burlap sack. When Grandma Katy dumped it out, she saw it was mostly junk—except for a pair of hockey skates. According to family lore,

Dad had to fight his sister Edna for ownership of those skates. But once they were his, the seeds were sown for the greatest career in the history of the game. Dad was six years old. He wore those skates for the next four years straight. Incredible how the Good Lord repays kindness exponentially.

Dad never forgot my grandmother's generous heart. Nor the benevolence of countless other friends and neighbors in Saskatoon who helped him keep his date with destiny. Mr. Hockey gave whole-heartedly. When I was about ten years old, he told me a story and asked me to keep it between the two of us—which I did, until now. (Sorry, Dad, but I think the world will benefit from knowing.) Near the end of Dad's 1952–53 season, he had forty-nine goals. The only NHL player ever to score fifty goals was his fierce rival, Maurice "Rocket" Richard. Dad was hoping to reach that coveted milestone and, God willing, surpass it. The Good Lord came through. In one of the last games of the year, Mr. Hockey was parked in front of the opposing net. A shot came in from the point, deflected off his big arse (Dad's words), and sailed into the net.

Not only was this a huge milestone, but it meant a big bonus. Dad could put that money to good use, perhaps even buy a second car so mom didn't have to ask the neighbors to drive her to get groceries. Mr. Hockey celebrated the way he usually did. A modestly raised stick. A subtle grin. He circled back toward his teammates, expecting to be mobbed for accomplishing such a rare feat. But they were mobbing the player who took the shot. Everyone assumed the goal was the defenseman's. It would have been the point man's twentieth, which meant a significant bonus for him as well. Instead of setting the record straight, Dad just joined the celebration. And that was that.

That's what I mean by whole-heartedly. Dad never did anything grudgingly or for show. If he did something for you it was because he wanted to. He was the most unselfish player I've ever seen. How many times did he have an open net for an easy goal but passed the puck to his teammate instead of shooting? And after the game was over, how many millions of dollars' worth of sticks, jerseys, pucks, skates, and other equipment did he give away to trainers, coaches, teammates, and friends? If you asked for it, it was yours.

Often he handed it to you before you asked. The night watchman at Olympia Stadium was mugged and robbed of his watch during a Red Wings game in the late sixties. The moment Dad learned of this, he removed his priceless Wings wristwatch and handed it to the speechless guard. "This is between you and me," Dad instructed. Of course the watchman couldn't contain his excitement, and soon the press learned of Dad's gesture. Mr. Hockey received a dozen watches anonymously over the next few days.

On the other hand, good luck trying to get something away from Gordie Howe if he'd decided he was going to keep it. You wouldn't get very far trying to strong-arm a farm boy from Saskatoon. Near the end of Dad's career, he achieved one of his most remarkable milestones, notching his thousandth assist. He'd promised the prized milestone stick to his good friend Chuck Robertson. But the moment the game ended, a Hockey Hall of Fame representative swooped into the change room while my dad was half-undressed and requested the stick.

"I'm sorry, I already promised it to a friend," Mr. Hockey informed him.

"It belongs in the Hall of Fame," the representative persisted.

Dad acquiesced. He grabbed the stick from the rack and grudgingly handed it to the representative, who left in triumph. Little did he know that what my dad had given him was another stick off the rack. The milestone stick was destined for Chuck Robertson.

For many years the counterfeit stick was displayed at the Hockey Hall of Fame, with no one the wiser, except Chuck and Dad.

—

Mr. Hockey was generous with others, but he never seemed to buy anything for himself. Mom took him shopping when it was time for new clothes, a new car, or a new house. If he wanted fishing gear or golf clubs . . . well, they tended to just materialize. Which actually happened frequently. If he did an appearance or a charity event, the sponsors would try to pay him. He typically told them to give the money back to the charity. If they insisted, he'd say, "Well, I could use a nice fishing rod." Hence, we had a lot of top-shelf fishing gear and sets of golf clubs in our garage—most of them monogrammed "GH."

But my father's indifference to money cut both ways.

He was criticized by some for not jumping on the bandwagon to unionize NHL players back in the fifties. As I understand it, Dad's iconic linemate and close friend, Ted Lindsay, and a few other financially savvy players recognized that the NHL owners were taking advantage of them and the players attempted to strengthen their position by forming a players' union. But it wasn't in Mr. Hockey's nature to ask for more. He was ecstatic just to be playing the game he loved so much. So he declined to sign on, and the union faltered.

Much later, in 1968, Dad's new teammate and friend Bobby Baun broke ranks and informed Mr. Hockey that two players on the Wings were being paid almost double what he was. Wings management had always told Dad that he was the highest-paid player in the league. He was gutted—but not because he had missed out on so much money for so many years. Rather, he was hurt that the team he had given so much to had betrayed him for over two decades.

However, I believe that Mr. Hockey's Boy Scout attitude is what set him apart. For him, it had never been about the money. It was about doing his best, doing what he loved, and treating people well. Sure, some people cheated him. But in the end, a cheater robs himself most of all. You can't love money and love people too. If you feel you have to cheat to get ahead, you've already lost.

Several people have said to me, "It's a shame your dad was so poorly paid for most of his career." I look at it differently. To me it was a blessing. Mr. Hockey *was* Mr. Hockey because he remained hungry, focused, and alive. He never thought he was special. Dad never once lamented that he should have been paid more. Money meant nothing to him—except as something to give away. Gordie Howe lived to give. In his eyes, his time, talents, and treasures belonged to the world, not to him.

———

My parents were utterly devoted to my siblings and me. They didn't spoil us, however, and they made sure we understood the value of a dollar. I slowly began to grasp that if I wanted something, I had to earn it, or at least wait patiently for it.

When I was about nine, I saw a karate uniform advertised in *Boys' Life*, the official magazine of the Boy Scouts of America, and I wanted it *badly*. I showed the ad to my mom, and she said, "Hmm, maybe someday. But not now." So like most kids, I then went to Dad, hoping to get a better answer.

"Well, what did your mother say?" he cleverly inquired. He would never go against her wishes.

"Um, well, she was kind of, like . . . well, wondering what you thought about it," I stumbled.

"Then I'll talk to her about it later."

Shoot! I needed that outfit. Right then. I'm not sure why, but I was convinced that I did. So I sulked for several days. And pouted. Then sulked a little more. Eventually, I was all sulked out and forgot about it.

Six months later came Christmas. There was one package under the tree I just couldn't figure out. If given enough time to shake, squish, rattle, and thump, an experienced kid can identify the contents of a wrapped gift with pretty high accuracy. But this one . . . well, I had *no idea*.

I opened the gift, and sure enough, I was staring at the *baddest* silky blue satin karate uniform with black trim, a tiger emblem on the chest, and a *black belt*! It was actually a kung fu uniform, but what did I know? Anyway, I loved that outfit and could hardly be convinced to change out of it. And I felt so bad for acting like such a selfish, impatient spoiled brat. It was the perfect lesson for me: *good things come to those who wait*.

But you know, receiving something you covet never feels as

good as giving to someone else. Neighbors of ours had a cat they adored and were devastated it was killed on our street.

A few days later, my parents visited the local humane society and picked out the cutest, sweetest little kitten, placed him in a box decorated with his paw prints and a ribbon, and added a little note saying, "Hello, my name is Tigger, and I need a home. Would you help me?"

Mom and Dad instructed me and my siblings to sneak the box onto our neighbors' front porch, then ding-dong ditch them. We gladly complied. Then we watched from behind a car under the cover of night as they opened the door and said, "What's this? Ooh, it's a little kitten! Isn't he cute? Tigger! Hi, Tigger!"

As I think about this now, it was pretty presumptuous of my parents to give our grieving neighbors a new cat. Maybe they didn't *want* a new cat. We'll never know. But self-doubt was not in my parents' lexicon. No time for what-ifs. And that was just one more thing I loved about them.

———

My parents took us on vacation everywhere they went. They didn't have a lot of disposable income, so we typically stayed in low-budget motels and packed in however we could. One of the nicest places we stayed was Homosassa Springs, Florida. After the hockey season ended each year, many of the Wings players and their families piled into their beat-up old station wagons and made the twenty-hour trek south to unwind over Easter vacation. I always thought it was really nice of the Wings owner, Bruce Norris, to host the players at the resort he owned, Homosassa Springs.

It was a modest fifties-era resort motel situated in the heart of the ecologically unique freshwater springs that served as an ideal habitat for manatees, black bears, bobcats, alligators, waterbirds, and deer. The centerpiece of the resort was a zoological park where you could feed the gators marshmallows and meet T.V. celebrity animals such as Clarence the Cross-eyed Lion and Gentle Ben.

I found out later that Mr. Norris didn't pay for the rooms; he just "invited" the players to stay at his resort, on their own dime. I remember meeting him on only a handful of occasions. He was very tall, handsome, and always impeccably dressed, but he seemed to have difficulty relating to others, especially kids. I don't remember him ever smiling or actually saying a word to me or my siblings. He seemed to be a very lonely person, and I felt sorry for him.

Mom and Dad splurged on the Homosassa Springs trip for our benefit, and it was a great experience for players and their families. I distinctly remember the drinks at the resort's restaurant. These weren't your run-of-the-mill kiddie cocktails. These were umbrella-shaded concoctions artfully presented in tall glasses with translucent blue marlin stir sticks about eight inches long. I kept ordering more and more drinks so I could collect an entire school of marlin to play with in the bathtub and the pool. After three days of this, my mom confronted me poolside and asked, "Where did you get all those plastic fish?"

I proudly explained to her that these weren't just fish, these were marlins, and I got them with the free drinks at the restaurant. My mom took a deep breath, smiled, and calmly explained, "Honey, those drinks are *not* free." She informed me that I had racked up a king's ransom in debt on my parents' tab. Oops!

Despite the overpriced drinks, the experiences at Homosassa Springs were priceless. The players fished and golfed together while the moms congregated at the pool to drink tropical cocktails and make sure their kids didn't kill anyone or drown. Alex Delvecchio happened to have a son my age, Alex Junior. He and I spent our days looking for adventure around the resort. The local drugstore required us to drink our Coca-Colas on-site, and then demanded that we relinquish our bottles so that the store could keep the ten-cent return for themselves. Alex Jr. and I figured this was highway robbery, so that night we dressed in black from head to toe, and helped ourselves to the empty bottles piled high outside the store. We cashed them in the next morning for a buck fifty. Was it illegal to steal back our own dimes plus a premium for shipping and handling? Yes. Was it fun? You betcha.

Alex Junior and I also followed Red Berenson's cute little daughter all over the place, just to gawk at her. I believe her name was Kelly, but we were both too shy at the time to actually talk to her and find out if she had a name.

———

Tonight, while the house sleeps, I wish I could tell my parents one more time how grateful I am for all the trips they took us on.

Once the grandkids were born, my parents took them everywhere as well. Mostly without their parents. That way, we parents wouldn't know that my mom bought our kids ice cream three times a day. In 1992, my parents were invited to be guests at a hockey tournament in Moscow. Mom invited Mark's daughter, Azia (then eleven), and Cathy's daughter,

Jaime (twelve), to join them. The girls' fondest memory from that trip was of handing out bags and more bags of gum to people on the streets, since gum was at that time a highly valued Russian commodity. Mom and Dad were always about making others happy.

The following year, my parents asked Azia where she would like to go if she could go anywhere in the world. Azia didn't hesitate: "Hawaii!" Soon after, Mom and Dad were on an airplane with Azia, Jaime, Nolan, and Jade, en route to Oahu. Azia likes to recount her "turtle" story from that adventure. In Honolulu, it seems, Azia, Jaime, and my mom were snorkeling when Azia found herself face to face with two giant sea turtles. She panicked and made a beeline for the beach, latching on to Dad's legs upon reaching shore.

When she told my dad what had happened, he said, "They won't hurt you! C'mon, Nolan, let's go find the turtles!" They left Azia on the beach, grabbed their masks, and dove into the surf in search of turtles. But alas, the giants were gone. After that trip, my parents never let a birthday, holiday, or special occasion pass without buying Azia something that had to do with turtles. Every time she sees a turtle to this day, she still thinks of my parents and how generous they were.

For more than fifteen years, Mom and Dad also rented a condo in Siesta Keys, Florida, and invited the family to join them. Colleen and I wanted in on the ice cream, so we tagged along, but Mom was the ringleader. And Dad the driver. They whisked the grandkids away to cool day-trip destinations, including Sarasota Jungle Gardens, Busch Gardens Tampa, SeaWorld, and Disney World. At Siesta Dunes, my parents would walk the beach with the kids to teach them about seashells, starfish, and sand dollars, and Dad led most of the snorkeling excursions. He'd spend an afternoon handing out his day's haul of sand dollars to passersby. No one had it in them to inform him that he was single-handedly decimating the Gulf Coast's sand-dollar population.

Siesta Key was a popular destination for hockey players. My wife, Colleen, overheard a boy and his mom talking excitedly about seeing a hockey great at the pool. Coll chimed in, "Gordie Howe is my father-in-law. I could get his autograph for you, if you like."

The boy looked confused. "Who's Gordie Howe?" Turns out they were talking about legendary Michigan State hockey coach Ron Mason.

Mom piped up, "Oh well, honey, Gordie Howe is the greatest hockey player ever! You definitely want his autograph too!" For years after that whenever I wanted to get a rise out of Dad I'd say, "Aren't you that hockey player, Ron Mason?"

During the summer, Mom and Dad packed up picnic lunches and boated the kids over to Marion Island, just off the coast of Bowers Harbor in the West Bay of Michigan's Grand Traverse Bay. On the way, the kids water-skied and tubed—a harrowing experience with Dad flying over the West Bay whitecaps, which were almost always in force due to the prevailing west winds. Upon reaching the beach, bruised and battered, the kids often had the entire island to themselves for the day, leaving them free to explore, build sand castles, and search for Petoskey stones. The day would end with stargazing, a campfire, and s'mores, compliments of Grandma and Grandpa.

Back in Traverse City, my parents loved taking the grandkids on walks to church, to the Omelette Shoppe for their cinnamon rolls, and to Bardon's Ice Cream. Everywhere they went, they struck up extended conversations with the priest, reverend, waitress, or anyone else who happened to be within talking distance. They loved people, and they were very proud of their grandchildren and loved to introduce them.

Mr. Hockey also took the grandkids to the now defunct Arnie's Funland for go-karting, to the Clinch Park zoo to ride the mini train, to the fish ladder to watch the salmon leap their way up the Boardman River to spawn, and to the assortment of putt-putt golf courses. My parents didn't just idly sit by and watch the kids; they drove the go-karts, rode the train, and putt-putted. My dad tried to win every time they played mini golf, but Mom always fudged the scorecard at Pirates Cove so that one of the grandkids would emerge victorious.

Ironically, no matter how much my parents gave away, everything just kept coming back to them. In the early seventies, Lincoln-Mercury signed Dad to its sports panel, alongside the likes of Jesse Owens, Al Kaline, Bart Starr, Byron Nelson, Dave DeBusschere, Cale Yarborough, Tony Trabert, and Frank Gifford. As part of the deal, he received two free cars each year—even after my brother Mark totaled a brand-new Lincoln Town Car shortly after his sixteenth birthday.

Around that time, Dad also received a free boat from Chrysler. It was red and white, and all the Howe kids' names were painted on one side. Dad loved that boat, and spent countless days dragging us around the lake on our water skis and countless nights trolling for trout under the stars.

Remarkably, even in later years when Dad's memory began failing him, he never forgot to offer to pay for dinner, groceries, ice cream, and so on. He would not leave the house without his wallet. If the caregivers had forgotten to tuck it in his back pocket, he'd stop at the door on the way out, grab the rear of his pants, and make a face like "Where is it?" He'd then check to make sure it was still there every few minutes at the grocery store.

I eventually removed his credit card and driver's license from his wallet, fearing that he would give everything away to a stranger. We were at a memorial service a few years ago, and Dad was mucking around with a little tyke, maybe four years old. He wanted to give the boy an autographed photo, but I'd forgotten to bring any. Dad signed a napkin but wasn't satisfied with that. So he opened his wallet and handed the boy his Red Wings alumni membership card with his photo on it. I thought about stopping him, but then I realized, "This is what Dad wants to do. Let him do it. This will be the memento of a lifetime for this young man. Plus, Dad will still be able to get in the alumni room anytime he wants!"

Dad wanted everyone in the world to have his autograph. He knew how much joy it brought to them. He never felt comfortable charging to sign—unless the money was going to a charity—and he never cared that his autograph might be worth less if he signed everything. Everywhere we went, Dad was always armed with a bundle of pens. He'd sign hats, shirts, sticks, shoes, hockey bags, foreheads, forearms, necks, and hands. He drew the line if the request involved a body part that never saw daylight.

Everything of value he had, he'd try give to me: his favorite ball caps, his Red Wings sweaters and golf shirts, his Gordie Howe ties. I tried to explain that his stuff was three times too big for me, but he wouldn't take no for an answer.

So I'd graciously accept it, then sneak everything back into his closet after he went to sleep. He tried to give his prized gold watch to Pedro, one of his bodyguards. But Pedro already had his own gold wristwatch, a huge shiny timepiece about the size of a Chihuahua. Dad finally talked him into swapping watches for the day.

We all owe something to our parents. More than something—much closer to everything. The patient hours they spend, and the small (or large) fortunes. The guidance they give us and the great advice. Was I luckier than most? I don't know, as I've never had any other parents. But I know I was blessed. To say that I was fortunate to have such generous, caring, loving parents doesn't even begin to express the debt of gratitude I feel towards them. Not in a million years could I ever repay their kindness. But that won't keep me from trying to pay it forward.

If Dad ever found a coin on the ground, he'd never pocket it. Instead, he'd hand it to me and say, "Do something good with this."

3

Play Hard, but Have Fun

"If it's not fun, do something else."

It's 3:00 a.m. Colleen is still buried beneath her Pillow Mountain. She's oblivious to my incessant hunting and pecking on my keyboard, thank God. Riding a tidal wave of emotions, I'm not even remotely tired. I'm still reeling from the realization that I will never again be able to hug my dad in this world. He seemed immortal, and even though I knew his end was coming, it's difficult to grasp now that it's here.

I'm also staring face to face with my own mortality. I'm headed in the same direction as Dad in thirty years. Three decades is a blink of an eye from where I sit. I've been married longer than that. Actually, I would consider myself fortunate to have thirty more quality years, given all the ER cases I've seen as a physician. The distance between heaven and here is no thicker than a highway's centerline. Each night at work, I'm reminded of how quickly lives can be snuffed out by a head-on collision, cardiac arrest, stroke, ruptured aneurysm, or a blood clot in the lung.

But I sense Dad hovering over me right now. I feel his penetrating gaze. He's playing tiny violins made with his thumbs and index fingers, and the tune is called "Stop the Pity Party!" He's telling me, "You have so many blessings. Don't miss out on what's right in front of you. Savor the moment. Carpe the diem. Mom and I are fine. Now get out there and have some fun, before I get out my Northland and whack you in the back of the head!"

So I'm not going to spend another moment feeling sorry for myself. I'm going to be joyful, in Dad's honor. I can't think of anyone who was more joyful or playful; in fact, Dad's middle name, if his parents had given him one, would have been Playful. For Dad's eighty-sixth birthday, Wayne Gretzky, the Great One, called to wish him well, as he did every year. Mr. Hockey grabbed the receiver and said, "Whatever it is, I didn't do it!" He enjoyed every minute of his life, and he'd be disappointed if I didn't do the same.

He was truly a child at heart, and he identified with children the moment he saw them. He dazzled them by magically making a coin disappear, pulling his finger off, lifting them off the ground by their ears, or bringing them to their knees with a crushing handshake or tickle to the midsection. Remarkably, the kids could not get enough of this abuse. He couldn't either.

Dad was also famous for his on-ice antics. For starters, he began his warm-up by scooping up ice shavings with the blade of his stick and dumping them on a random (or sometimes not-so-random) fan. Even the officials and his opponents weren't immune from a good "icing." People loved it. Mr. Hockey always searched for those he thought would get the biggest rise, such as a little kid or someone in a wheelchair or on crutches who appreciated a boost. Sometimes he'd target an extremely well-dressed man or woman, as if to say, "Don't take yourself too seriously."

He did some other cool stuff during warm-ups, like firing a puck off the crossbar so that it would fly over the glass and land in the hands of some lucky fan. Dad the hockey magician could make that puck drop anywhere he wanted. The kid who caught it would jump up and down like he'd hit the jackpot. But there was a method to Dad's pregame frivolity: it kept him loose and relaxed. More importantly, as he told me once, it reminded him, "without the fans, the officials, and the opposing team, *there was no game.*" Everyone played an equally important role in Mr. Hockey's eyes.

My brother Mark told me that he learned the secret to Dad's hockey genius while sitting next to him on the bench in his first year with the Houston Aeros. Occasionally an unsuccessful puck clearing from the Aeros' zone resulted in a golden opportunity for an opposing defenseman: a puck slowly gliding along the boards and right onto his stick. He had all the time in the world to make a play. Sort of like a slow-moving grounder making its way toward a first baseman on a baseball diamond. An easy out.

But because it was so easy, the defenseman sometimes relaxed a bit and failed to position his body behind the puck as a safety net. He didn't think he'd need to. In these instances, Dad quietly whispered the word "jump" just as the puck reached the defenseman's stick blade. Wouldn't you know it, that damn puck hopped right over the player's stick and outside the zone almost every time, resulting in an offside call!

Dad's sense of humor could alleviate even the worst pain. Bill Gadsby was playing with the Red Wings around 1964, and he got nailed with a slap shot directly in his family jewels. He dropped to the ice and curled up in the fetal position, grimacing and gasping for breath.

My dad quickly skated over to help. "Bill," he shouted. "Bill!" Uncle Bill, as we called him, looked up at Mr. Hockey.

"Open your mouth," Dad instructed. Obviously, he'd had some experience with this kind of injury. Bill opened his mouth. My dad peered at him intently and said, "Yep, I see 'em!" That got Bill laughing so hard, it almost took away the pain.

Dad could be both playful and powerful at the same time. One player who could attest to this was Bryan Watson. Off the ice Bryan was a class act, but on the ice he was unhinged. Fiery and fearless. His intensity reminded me of Rocket Richard. He was known for his unbridled scrappiness in the corners and the slot, and his eagerness to drop his gloves at the first hint of trouble. Or even beforehand. He got into so many brawls that his face was covered with gashes that framed his flattened boxer's nose; he looked *exactly* like a thug for the Irish mob. That's why his nickname was Bugsy, or so I think.

Anyway, after Bryan was traded to the Wings in 1965, Dad and Bugsy became good friends—they admired each other's toughness, off-color humor, and ability to smack a golf ball out of sight. Bugsy frequently found himself grilling steaks poolside in our backyard after tearing up the links with Mr. Hockey. But in 1967, Bryan was traded from the Wings and eventually ended up with the Oakland Seals. It was awkward to see my dad playing against his friend whenever Oakland came into town. One particular game devolved into a series of donnybrooks, and Dad and Bugsy found themselves on the ice together when yet another scuffle broke out.

The unwritten rule in hockey is that when a fight breaks out, everyone "has a man"—that way, there's less risk of someone getting ganged up on. But the Wings were killing a penalty at the time, and they had only four skaters on the ice to the Seals' five. Bugsy was going at it with someone (surprise, surprise), and my dad had also paired off, but there was still a loose Seal roaming around the ice. So Dad *dragged* the guy he'd paired off with over to the lone skater and collared both of them, scrunching the two Seals together like a father reprimanding his sons. The crowd roared. Finally, the other fights subsided, and Mr. Hockey released his catch.

Later in the game, Bugsy found himself in another drawn-out skirmish. The refs let Bryan and the Red Wing go at it for a bit, but Dad was getting impatient. Taking matters into his own hands, he dove in between the two players, pushed his teammate away, and grabbed Bryan in a viselike headlock.

So there they were, two good friends, with Mr. Hockey down on one knee and Bryan's head collared by the strongest force known to man, or at least known to me—my father's arm. Dad said something to him like, "Okay, Bryan, I'm getting *really* hungry and you're making this game go on forever. Let's finish it so we can go get a steak." Dad then released his grip, and he and Bugsy headed to the penalty box together, still continuing their friendly conversation. We all went out to eat afterward, and my dad and Bryan had a good laugh.

Dad's pranking skills were popular with his teammates. If a player was engrossed in a good book, Dad or one of his co-conspirators would wait until he was near the end and then secretly tear out the last page. They would let the other members of the team in on the joke and then wait until the "target" was about to turn to the last page. Inevitably, the reader would stand up in the plane and shout, "All right, who's the %$*&^*#% who took the end of my book?" and the entire plane would erupt in laughter. The page would be returned, sooner or later, so it could be taped in place before the book was taken back to the local public library.

The players always had a lot of downtime in airport terminals, waiting for flights. When he wasn't tackling a crossword puzzle, Dad loved euchre, bridge, and poker. When he tired of cards, he and his teammates would attach fishing line to a five-dollar bill and place it invitingly on the floor for a traveler to "bite." The moment a victim bent down to grab it, one of the players would yank the line just a few inches. Then the entire peanut gallery would erupt with laughter, embarrassing the victim, who would sometimes try to grab the bill and run, but usually just blushed and hurried away. Dad liked to catch up and reward the traveler with a handshake.

After games or practices, Mr. Hockey was also an expert at putting things like salt tabs in a teammate's shoes, hiding a coveted piece of a player's gear, or stealthily deposting a slush ball (wiped from his skate blade) down the back of a teammate's neck. Dad just loved getting a rise out of people. It was his way of showing he cared.

Outside the arena, Dad savored each moment of every day, enjoying himself immensely whether he was driving to the grocery store, shoveling snow, or grilling burgers. He insisted that life should be fun, and that if you didn't enjoy what you were doing, you should do something else.

He never took himself, nor anyone else, too seriously. He was never at a loss for something funny to say or do. He used to stick out his false teeth at the dinner table, much to the chagrin of my mom, but to the delight of all the kids. He also used to hide our food if any of us looked away for a moment. We learned to keep one hand on our plates at all times.

If you were a kid asking for an autograph, he'd point to your shirt and ask you what was on it; when you looked down, he'd tag your nose with his finger. "Gotcha!" he'd say and laugh right along with you.

If he was signing an autograph, he'd deftly tattoo the fan's hand or nose before the kid knew what hit him. "Oops, I slipped," he'd quip. I'm amazed he never skewered anyone's eyeball.

Mr. Hockey also loved to pick kids up "by their ears"—which meant he grabbed their ears, while the kids reflexively grabbed his forearms. He hoisted them up until he sensed they were losing their grip and then gently lowered them down. Sometimes he'd hold his hands under their armpits and swing them like a human pendulum, and when they got high enough, he'd flip them all the way over. This worked well most of the time, but on a few occasions he got drilled in the face by an errant boot, so he learned to hold his head back at a safe distance.

He sparred openhanded with little boys until they grew tired of being tagged, and then he'd just hold them in a headlock until my mom noticed that they were turning blue. She'd gently observe, "He's suffocating, Gordie." But the boys loved it and would come back for more.

Just to get kids riled up, he *loved* addressing the boys with girls' names and vice versa. "Oh hello, Sally," he'd say to a rough-and-tumble seven-year-old boy in a hockey jacket.

The boy would be indignant. "I am *not* a GIRL!" he'd protest. "My name is Bill!"

"Jill?" Dad would say, feigning an apologetic face. "Oh, I am sorry."

By this time, steam would be escaping from little Billy's beet-red ears. "Bill! My name is Bill!"

"Ohhhhhhh, Billllllllllll. Well, why didn't you just say so?"

Terry Sawchuk's son Jerry played with Dad in a Red Wings old-timers game in Port Huron, Michigan, many years ago. Dad hadn't seen Jerry for decades, but he caught the SAWCHUK on the back of his jersey when they both found themselves in the bathroom. Suddenly Jerry felt a stick hook him around the neck. "How's it going, Mary?" Dad ribbed. That had been his nickname for Jerry when he was a little kid.

Mr. Hockey's sense of humor was often beyond irreverent, and completely unpredictable. In the mid-eighties, my parents befriended Craig MacFarlane, the renowned blind Canadian super-athlete. Craig, who was then nineteen, had made a name for himself as a championship wrestler, and he'd set numerous world records for blind athletes. He had a tremendous sense of humor, a huge smile, good looks, and *no fear*. There was nothing he wouldn't try.

My parents immediately hit it off with Craig, and they invited him to move in with them for a time so they could help him promote his career. During his stay, we brought him up to our family cabin in Michigan. I asked him if he'd ever water-skied. He said, "No, but I'll try it!" Randy Omer, our close family friend, my dad, myself, and Randy's youngest son, Lance, showed him the ropes. He got up on two skis his first try, and skied around the entire lake, finishing with a grand splash in front of our beach. Everyone on the dock cheered loudly, as they always did for a first-timer, sighted or otherwise. Just to be funny I said to Craig, "You should try the ski jump! It's right in front of you!" Randy was the only guy I ever met who felt the need to have a 25-foot-long ski ramp in front of his cabin. This was a huge, professional ramp you'd only find at a water ski show. Randy made sure everyone tried it at least once. I'd done it many times, and it terrified me every time. Dad went off it once, sideways, but lived to tell the tale.

Craig said "Hell yeah, I'll try it!" We all thought he was crazy, but we also wanted to witness history, so Lance drove the boat, and Randy skied alongside him to tell him where the ramp was. Craig hit that ramp and soared like an eagle for a good forty feet. He then lost control and face-planted, but bobbed back up shouting, "Let's go again!" It was the most courageous feat I'd ever seen. He nailed it on his second try.

Shortly after that, Craig moved to Florida and became a professional water-skier at Cypress Gardens. Unbelievable. Dad loved Craig's indomitable spirit, and nicknamed him "The Bat."

———

If you've played much hockey, you've probably noticed that the toughest guys are also often the funniest. Maybe a sense of humor comes more easily to people who are harder to intimidate. Or maybe it works the other way—maybe it's harder to intimidate the guys who have a sense a humor.

In any case, at a charity hockey tournament a few years ago, I had the pleasure of having breakfast with Tiger Williams, the all-time NHL leader in penalty minutes and one of the toughest men I've ever met. He told me that he had once played in a charity game that pitted NHL alumni, including Mr. Hockey, against a number of actors known as the Hollywood Stars. Tiger faced off against Jason Priestley, a Vancouver native and one of the heart-throbs of *Beverly Hills, 90210*. Jason rubbed Tiger the wrong way—according to Tiger, "He was just too %^$& good-looking." So just to be funny, he rode the actor out along the boards and gently squished his perfectly chiseled face against the glass. Tiger then whispered in his ear, "If you touch the puck again, I'm going to %&^$* your $%^& face!" Jason wasn't sure if Tiger was kidding or not.

The combination of humor and toughness was Dad's signature, and it turned out to be multi-generational. When our oldest son, Gordie, was about ten, I was his hockey coach. We had a big player on our team—a head taller than Gordie who just seemed to have my son's number. In practice scrimmages, he repeatedly cross-checked and tripped Gord for no reason. I told the player to knock it off, but he persisted, and one day during practice, Gordie decided he'd had enough.

The boy had just cross-checked him in the back, unprovoked; the puck was nowhere near the two of them. Gord got back on his feet, grabbed his stick with both hands, and raised it high overhead. This wasn't going to end well. I shouted, "GOOOOO RRRRRRRRRRDIIIIIIIIIIIIIIIIE!" and he eased up mid swing, so that his stick plunked lightly onto the top of the player's helmet and shoulder, rather than bisecting him. The kid had seen what was coming, and it scared the stuffing out of him.

I gave Gord a short time-out on the bench to cool his jets, then I pulled the other kid aside and explained to him that if he kept bothering my son, I couldn't be held responsible for what he might do. (Technically, I could, but I figured the kid wouldn't know that at the age of ten.)

On the way home from practice, Mr. Hockey broke the silence in the car. "So, Gordie," he said, "it looked like that big kid was bugging you out there, eh?"

Young Gordie nodded. He was still ticked off.

My dad just stared out the window and muttered, "I guess he won't be bugging you anymore, will he?"

Gordie grinned widely and chuckled, "No, I guess not!"

My two Gordies, sharing a moment of mayhem. I guess this was genetic.

Dad was nothing if not consistent. As a grade-schooler, my brother Marty always took his time getting home from school every day. He'd linger to flirt with the girls, and like Dad, he just never seemed to rush anywhere. Mark, on the other hand, prided himself in getting home first. But one day, Mark got home and Marty was already sitting at the table. Just then, Mom came down and read Marty the riot act for being kicked out of school for fighting. Apparently, the kid who sat behind him in class didn't know when to stop taunting, "Gordie Howe sucks. Red Wings suck." Marty pounded him.

When Dad came home, Mom chided him for teaching his sons to be violent. He waited until she left the room, then whispered, "Good job, Marty!"

Even Dad's healthcare providers weren't immune. His primary care doctor was the world-renowned sports medicine physician Dr. Roger Kruse.

Dr. Kruse stepped in the room. "Good to see you, Mr. Howe."

Without missing a beat, Dad looked up at him and said, "Yeah, I'm sure it is. You just want to feel my balls again!"

After composing himself, Dr. Kruse then proceeded to resect a sizeable lump on Dad's shin. Using a razor-sharp scalpel and a little lidocaine, Roger sliced off a skin tumor the size of a small rodent. Blood gushed everywhere. Mr. Hockey never flinched. But then suddenly he grimaced and howled, "Owwwwwwwwwwwwww!"

Dr. Kruse recoiled. "I'm sorry, Mr. Howe! Am I hurting you?"

My dad laughed and said, "No, but I gotcha, didn't I?"

———

Looking back over my life, the best times with my father were those quiet moments when the two of us were really able to talk. These memories are pure gold to me. If there is one piece of advice I would give to any parent, it is to make some one-on-one time with each kid on a regular basis. It can be something as simple as sharing a meal or a walk together. No smartphone, tablet, or television. Just the two of you spending time together. These are the moments when you really have a chance to bare your souls and truly come to know each other.

My earliest memory of male bonding with my dad was when we took a fishing trip to an unnamed lake in Ontario, somewhere north of Sault Ste. Marie, when I was nine. Dad and I were traveling with Randy Omer and his eldest son, Robin. We drove over eight hours to get there and stayed in the *only* cabin on the lake. It was as peaceful, serene, and solitary as it gets—and cold. Although it was late June, we woke up with frost on our noses. But after we'd fired up the wood-burning stove and heated up some hot chocolate and oatmeal to warm our bellies, we were as toasty as geckos in Guam.

After breakfast, Dad and I headed out in a little boat equipped with a handheld five-horsepower outboard. We trolled along for a good half hour until my dad found a spot that seemed just right and anchored. I was always amazed at how Mr. Hockey just "knew" when he was in the right fishing spot.

And for the next eight hours, we talked. And sang songs, even though we didn't know the words. It was always "something, something, CHORUS, something, hmm, hmmm, CHORUS, something, hmmmm, hmmmm, something, CHORUS CHORUS CHORUS."

We headed to a clearing on the shore, ate peanut butter and jelly sandwiches and apples, and drank more hot chocolate. We watered a few nearby trees. Then we sat on a log and talked some more. We talked about what Dad's life was like when he was a kid. And about his mom, whom he loved so dearly. And about all the people in Saskatoon who had inspired him or been kind to him. Then he described Saskatoon as only Gordie Howe could: "It's so flat, you can watch your dog run away for three days."

We talked about my mom and my sister and girls in general. We decided that there was no figuring them out. You just had to appreciate all the wonderful things that made them who they were. There was certainly no changing them. We also talked about philosophy, religion, and the meaning of life. Mr. Hockey was a man of few words, but he had astonishing wisdom. One of his favorite expressions was "It doesn't cost anything to be nice to someone."

I can hardly remember if we caught any fish that day, but it seems to me that a few trout ended up in our frying pan for dinner. Fresh pan-fried rainbow are tough to beat. What I do remember for sure is that for my dad, enjoying life and taking it seriously were not two different things. Living each day to its fullest was as much a part of his philosophy as living honorably and living generously. They were all the same thing. He might have just called it being nice, but it gave him as much joy as a good joke or a day at the lake.

That is truly living life to its fullest.

After dinner, we sat around the campfire with Randy and Robin, swapping tall tales of the fish that "got away" that day. We played a few cards, and by nine o'clock we were sleeping like bears. We did it all again the following day, and on the third day, we reluctantly headed home. It was way too short, but oh so sweet.

In the darkness of my quiet house, those summer days are even sweeter now, all these years later.

———

The year after that trip, my dad and I were invited to go canoeing on the gorgeous but unforgiving Pine River, which runs through the Manistee National Forest in the northwestern part of the Michigan mitten. The trip was planned by a naturalist who each year led a small group on a three-day expedition down the pristine waterway.

The naturalist met up with us at the headwaters of the Pine, upstream from the Ne-Bo-Shone wilderness. He handed us each a bag of food about the size of a baseball and said, "This is your food for the next three days. The rest you will have to find." We stared at each other, and I'm sure we all had the same thought: "Run to the grocery store now!" But it was too late. The canoes were in the water. We said goodbye to civilization, warm food, and restrooms.

I was in a canoe with Dad. This was challenging enough, as a man that big makes any canoe innately unstable. Especially when he's all torso. Our center of gravity was about five feet above the water. To make matters worse, it had rained the previous four days straight, and the river was dangerously high. Class one rapids had become class two plus as the river raced relentlessly toward Lake Michigan.

As we fought our way through the frothy current, Dad and I talked a lot, but much of the conversation consisted of "Paddle left, left, left!" or "Duck!" We capsized a lot the first two days, trying to navigate the rapids. I was in front, and my job was to call out which direction we needed to head as we negotiated the water hazards. But I was usually a second too late, and time and again, we crashed into assorted boulders and logs, spun sideways, and flipped. Then it was a floating yard sale of paddles, water bottles, unworn life jackets, and dry bags containing food, tents, sleeping bags, and clothes. Dad had no desire to be swimming in these rapids. Every time we collided with a boulder, he laughed and cursed at the same time, shouting, "Murray, what the dirtyrottenfritzofratz are you doing?"

We went for a few unplanned swims and lived to tell the tale. Mr. Hockey was very glad to survive and get off the river that day, although I'd never heard him laugh so hard and so often in one day. Mostly the laughter was at the end of each rapid, when we realized that we were still alive.

We didn't care about anything but our food bag. On at least one occasion, my dad yelled for me to grab it as it rushed past. I nabbed it, gulping a few mouthfuls of cold Pine River as I flailed to get back to shallower water. It was worth it. The food bag was basically a wad of peanut butter and some gorp, but it was precious to us.

On the third day we rowed again. By then, we'd mastered padding our craft, so our conversation morphed from shouting panicked commands to singing unknown song lyrics again and talking about girls some more. It was a beautiful day and the perfect ending to a great trip. When we were back at our vehicle, we thanked our guide for the amazing experience, and then Dad hit the accelerator and hightailed it to the first building that resembled a restaurant. We downed a bucket of burgers within minutes.

I remember feeling how fortunate I was to be spending time alone with my dad. I loved seeing the twinkle in his eye, and the boyish grin as he recounted a funny story, and hearing his insights into life. I cherished his endless playlist of unintelligible songs hummed and faintly crooned between sips of his chocolate shake. This was a man who loved life and knew how to have fun with nothing more than a fishing rod, a paddle, or a pair of hiking boots.

That day, he told me, "Do what you love. You can't go wrong with that." It was clear that he didn't care whether I was a hockey player, a writer, or an adventure tour guide. He loved me purely because I was his son, and his joy came from knowing that I was happy.

I promised myself that if and when I had children of my own, I would carve out time alone with each of them, preferably somewhere off the grid, to truly get to know them and let them know that I love them unconditionally. I realized that the most valuable treasure in this world is the relationships we forge with others, and the experiences we share. Money, status, and fame—that all sounds good, but it pales in comparison to time well spent with someone you love.

———

Another great bonding experience with my happy-go-lucky father was our world-class salmon-fishing trip to the Peregrine Lodge in Northern British Columbia's remote Haida Gwaii Islands, off the southern tip of Alaska. Several years ago, my uncle Vic, my dad, and I were guests of the Toigo family. Ron Toigo, the majority owner of the Vancouver Giants junior hockey team, his family, and many of his close friends had also made the trek to this remote outpost, first by jet, then by helicopter.

The lodge was cozy and rustic, with an inviting stone fireplace and deliciously fragrant knotty-pine walls. But this was definitely not Disney's Fort Wilderness. Ferocious-looking fish and eel-like creatures were mounted on the walls. Outside, dragonflies the size of flying squirrels flitted here and there. Either way, the resort seemed to be a haven for extra-large wildlife, including Kodiak bears, moose, elks, whales, orcas, and other critters big enough to eat you.

The fish were also unusually large. The king salmon ran upward of seventy pounds, and the halibut could tip the scales at over three hundred. Halibut are as ugly as they are huge. Their entire faces are squashed over to one side of their bodies. These fish are living proof of God's sense of humor.

Fishing for these beauties was no small matter. My dad, Vic, and I, along with our guide, motored out in a trophy boat, a nice twenty-five-foot vessel with a twenty-foot "tuna tower" that would be the envy of any boater in Michigan. But our boats were like toys in those rough Alaskan waters. The boat in front of us disappeared between each thirty-foot swell. This roller coaster tested even the most seasoned sailor.

It was right about then that we understood why each of the fishermen was required to wear a survival suit. The suits allowed you to survive for more than twenty minutes if your boat sank, or if you fell overboard while relieving yourself.

I sensed this was a nightmare waiting to happen, since I had to keep an eye on two huge men, both well into their eighties. Neither of them was that sure-footed, particularly on a boat swaying in chaotic swells, and I was absolutely paranoid that my dad would be tossed into the drink and swept away. Anytime he was remotely near the edge of the boat, I had what I hoped was a firm hold of the back of his jacket. We would be going in together, I imagined. He kept giving me "the look"—the one that said he wasn't three years old and could handle himself just fine. I'm sure that was the case, but I wasn't taking any chances.

We finally reached the "perfect spot," where we fished for three hours without a bite. The guide then took us to a better "perfect spot," where we nabbed not even a nibble for an hour. But then, finally, Dad broke the slump, hooking a nice fifty-pounder, and then another. Then another. Whenever my dad fished, he always caught more than his share, using his fish magnetism. It was uncanny.

Uncle Vic and I stared at each other as if to say, "What's he doing that we aren't?" But after Dad had caught his limit, Vic and I finally hooked a few thirty-five-pounders that were great eating fish. Dad's bigger salmon looked impressive, but they'd taste like canned tuna.

The next day was even rougher. Vic elected to stay back at the lodge, but not Mr. Hockey. If there were any fish left in that ocean, he was going after them. I would have been happy to stay at the lodge, but if Mr. Hockey could do it, I could too. We took a beating just getting out there. The waves were relentless. But the beating was worth it, as this time when we found our "perfect spot," the salmon were literally jumping into the boat—probably to get out of the crashing seas.

In no time at all, Mr. Hockey landed three nice-sized kings. But then our luck ran out. For the next few hours, we were tossed around in the boat, and I felt my breakfast pleading with my esophagus to let it out. I finally cried "uncle" and said, "Dad, do you mind if we head in? I am going to hurl any second; these waves are destroying me!"

He put his massive arm around me and said with a smile, "I thought you'd never ask!" Mr. Hockey would never give in first.

———

The connection between toughness and good humor was never clearer than in Dad's later years. Just a few years ago, he and I, along with my son Gordie and our good friend Dale Saip, hopped a sea plane to the remote Twin Falls Lodge in Northern Saskatchewan for a few days of Walleye fishing.

The first day I decided to take Dad on a hike to the famous Robertson and Twin Falls on the Churchill River. The view of the thunderous waterfall was breathtaking, and on the hike back I remember thinking, "I will never forget this day!" I was right, but for a different reason.

A moment later, Dad, who had decided to take the lead, stepped off the edge of a cliff at the trail's edge, which was hidden by ferns. He simply vanished. The cliff was a 60-degree plummet, and I watched helplessly as he "log rolled" a good twenty feet down through stumps and rocks. Finally, his ribs slammed into a pair of soft birch trees that were strong enough to catch him, but not strong enough to kill him. If it weren't for those trees, he would have plummeted another ten feet straight into the rocks jutting out along the shoreline, and then dumped into the water. It would have surely killed him.

By the time I reached him, his arms were drenched in blood. He looked like a bomb victim. I looked him in the eyes to see what was left, and his gaze seemed to be saying "Whatareyoutryingtodotome?"

I laughed, overjoyed that he was still alive, and laughed at myself for the ridiculous situation that I'd put us in. I gave him a quick medical once-over. Remarkably, Dad seemed to have no life-threatening injuries, but his arms were shredded. I ripped my t-shirt in half and wrapped up his forearms—when I was done they looked like crimson NBA shooter sleeves.

It would be hours before anyone might find us, and there was no safe way to swim back along the rocky coastline, so we had to climb back up that twenty-foot steep hill.

I willed Dad's 220-pound frame upwards, inch by inch, root by root. Several times he tried to stand, teetering precariously and almost toppling backwards. By the grace of God, we made it to the top in about fifteen minutes. He then managed to hobble and wobble the rest of the way back to the lodge under his own power.

Ron Cojocar, the lodge manager, just about had a heart attack when he saw Dad, but helped me clean and dress his wounds, using up his entire supply of bandages from the first aid kit. The entire lodge crew slowly filtered in to hear the story and gawk at Dad's wounds. Despite everything he'd just been through, Mr. Hockey was in the best of spirits. One of the old-timers, John Rempel, said, "Well, with all your injuries, now would be about the only time in history I could take you on!"

In a heartbeat Dad had Mr. Rempel in a friendly headlock and chuckled, "I'm not dead yet."

By morning, the bleeding was down to a barely perceptible ooze. I suggested that maybe he wouldn't want to go fishing with his arms in that condition, but he smiled broadly and said, "*I'm* going fishing. Are you coming?"

———

In his later years, Dad's short-term memory was, as he put it, "in the toilet," but he never forgot how to be funny. Early in 2014, we went out to eat at Chandler Café, one of Dad's favorite Sylvania eateries. After the meal, he said he needed to use the bathroom. I escorted him to the men's room and asked if he needed help. His hands were so big and arthritic that it was getting hard for him to negotiate all the zippers, buttons, snaps, bells, and whistles. But he just gave me his usual roll of the eyes and said, "It's big enough. I can find it."

That spring on a hike near our home, we walked past the beautiful campus of Lourdes University. After I told him about the history of the university, he quipped, "This is the closest I've gotten to college."

My wife, Colleen, greeted my dad when he came down for breakfast one morning in the summer of 2014. "How are you feeling this morning, Gordie?" she asked. My dad just laughed and said, "With my hands," and went back to rummaging through the pantry looking for cookies.

Later that week, Colleen had twenty yards of mulch delivered, which meant that my dad and I had our hands full. We shoveled for several hours in the hot sun, and then my dad wandered off to the backyard. My neighbor Dale stopped by to chat a moment, and as we stood in the front yard talking, my dad slipped into the house and sat down on the comfy couch in front of the parlor window so he could watch me work.

Dale saw him first, and my dad just put his index finger over his mouth as if to say "Shhhhh." Dale burst out laughing and said, "Check out your dad! He's hiding from you!"

Dad's cleverness never waned, and only after his death did I learn of his final prank. In September 2016, when our family traveled to Saskatoon to attend many events in Dad's memory, we dropped by his old school.

The current principal, Krista Sego, showed me a signed Gordie Howe jersey she had on display in the office, along with a Northland hockey stick whose donor had insisted it was Dad's. She confided in me that when my dad had visited a few years earlier, he informed her that the stick was not his but his brother Vic's, because it was "curved the wrong way."

I examined the stick closely. It was Dad's patented Northland, taped in his unmistakable style, signed by him, and curved *right* (Dad was ambidextrous, but preferentially a right-hander). The stick was absolutely Mr. Hockey's. It seemed like a pretty good reminder that Dad could turn anything into a joke. Especially if you were a principal, you always had to look out for that twinkle in his eye.

4

Patience, Patience, Patience

"Take your time and do it right."

It's now shortly after 4:00 a.m., and I'm still wide awake. Dad pulled many all-nighters, traveling to where he was needed, be it Moncton, New Brunswick, or La Ronge, Saskatchewan. If he had an appearance he would be there, and on time, with a smile, no matter how many planes, trains, and automobiles were required. When I was eleven I watched him drive for twenty hours straight from Detroit to Miami. From my scrunched up position in the backseat of our 1972 Lincoln Continental, I awoke from time to time to check the rear view mirror to make sure Dad was still alert during the early morning hours. His massive fingers curled gently around the steering wheel, turning it with one finger at a time. His head never bobbed and his smile never faded as he lip-synched to the Sly and the Family Stone belting out "Dance to the Music" over and over and over again on the eight track. Dad never complained. Whatever the task at hand, he viewed it as an adventure and a privilege; never a chore.

"If he could do it, I can do it," I think to myself. I'm encouraged because the eulogy is taking shape nicely. The memories, the lessons—they are Dad. The stories rush over me ever more intensely, and I'm being swept away. The tears are soon overtaken by an uncontainable smile and laughter. Dad was something else. There was nobody like him.

One of the traits I most admired (and aspired to emulate) was his perpetual, impenetrable calm. How do you live for eighty-eight years without ever raising your voice? Try not raising your voice or losing your cool for even *one day*. Then you begin to realize how remarkable a man Mr. Hockey was. Living with someone like that makes you feel silly anytime you lose your cool.

But that particular trait is a double-edged sword. Mom used to get frustrated with Dad when she was really angry about something. "Why don't you ever get angry?" she'd exclaim. Dad would just shrug his massive shoulders and say, "Why should I?"

One reason my childhood was so nurturing was that I never had to worry that my dad would be upset. About anything. Once when I was about seven, I dumped over a huge glass of chocolate milk at the dinner table. For some reason, Mom wasn't home—which was good, because most moms I knew tended to freak out over spilt milk. (Probably because they knew that the house was going to smell like old cheese in about a week.) But Dad just laughed and said, "Hmmm, looks like you've got some work to do!" And he helped me clean it up.

Occasionally he'd be the one to drive me to my hockey practice or game. That was a huge treat. He'd make sure we were ready to leave waaaaaaaaay ahead of schedule so there'd be no need to rush. Five minutes before liftoff, he'd be helping me pack my equipment and load it into the station wagon. That way, he knew it would happen. And it was easier than shouting out orders and then wondering if I was doing what I was told. Dad was smart.

If he didn't know where I was in our home, he'd never yell for me. He'd quietly walk around the house until he found me. He'd appear out of nowhere like the Cheshire Cat, sometimes scaring the crap out of me. I think he did that on purpose.

Dad's calm nature explains why, if any of us kids got sick or injured, he would barely raise an eyebrow unless he saw blood spurting from a vital organ. The only time he ever seemed worried was when my brother Mark impaled himself on a hockey net. The center of the base of the net buried itself six inches into Mark's butt cheek, barely missing his rectum, and when Mark pushed off the net, about a pint of blood splattered across the goal crease. Arterial blood. Dad did rush down to be with him that time. (Fortunately, Mark was transported to the hospital and then the operating room lickety-split, and he made a full recovery. Mark's injury actually prompted an historic change in the design of hockey nets. The base of a net is now a U-shape instead of a W, eliminating the risk of impalement should the net tilt backward.)

Even though our father didn't get too excited about our ailments, he was very compassionate. I have vivid recollections of an ill-fated seaplane trip our family took in 1965 to Northern Ontario for a true Canadian wilderness adventure. After a few dips and sharply banked turns in that little plane, I suddenly didn't feel so good. I unbuckled and woozily navigated my way up to my mom and dad's seats and said, "I think I'm gonna be sick!"

Dad immediately scooped me up into his arms and said, "Muzz, you're gonna be fine. Just sit in my lap right here and look out that window!" I peered through the cockpit and out the front window. Although I was transfixed by the emerald-green lakes and boreal forest around us—not to mention the legions of switches, knobs, gauges, buttons, and levers almost close enough for me to touch—my mind couldn't shake the fact that my stomach felt like a caged raccoon that wanted to escape.

"Dad, I think I'm gonna barf!" I insisted. I was no medical expert (then), but based on my past barfing experiences, I was pretty sure this was not a drill. Dad smiled and gave me an encouraging rub on my buzzed head. "You're gonna be fine, Mur. We're almost there. Just keep looking out that window."

I looked out the cockpit window again. Nothing but endless forest and lakes. We were in the middle of nowhere, and it looked to me like we might be flying for hours before we found civilization. I sat up and puked all over my dad's stylish cardigan. Gordie Howe was then covered in barf. Then I puked again, on his lap. And again, on his sweater.

But Dad didn't jump up or hold me away from him. He accepted the vomit gracefully, and continued holding me in his arms.

"How do you feel now, Mur?" he said, chuckling.

"A lot better!" I announced.

Amazing how just a little barfing can bring so much joy. But of course Dad was drenched in puke, so I decided to traipse back to my clean seat. Not a drop of vomit on me. We landed about a minute later. Amazingly, he deplaned with a smile on his face, ready to meet the huge crowd of fans on the dock vying for position to meet a legend—a hero who was covered in puke.

Patience is the key to almost every facet of life, whether it's sports, your career, or how you relate to others. Patience seems to give you power over your world. It's an ability to accept the things you cannot change, and a confidence to prioritize and manage the things you can. With Dad, it was as if he had his own remote control.

With fans and friends, he prioritized whomever he was speaking with. He was going to make the moment count. He did the same thing with his teammates and his coaches. Each person had his undivided attention the moment they began a conversation. Ditto for the team trainer and physician. Mr. Hockey could recite verbatim whatever they told him.

Dad was the best listener I've ever known. "You have two eyes and one mouth," he liked to say. "If you want to learn something, keep one closed and the other two open."

In hockey, he was incredibly patient and poised whenever he carried the puck. He once told me, "Never just get rid of the puck. Hold on to it until you find something smart to do with it." He'd look for a decent shot, or try to set up a teammate. He'd never rush his move. If an opponent pressured him, Dad just used his imposing physique to shield the puck. I know this firsthand because except for maybe my brothers, I have played one on one against Gordie Howe more than anyone in the history of the game. Most of these skirmishes took place in our basement or driveway, but that still counts. Hockey is hockey.

My earliest recollection of playing hockey with Dad was in our driveway in our idyllic northwest Detroit suburb. The season stretched from March to November, but this particular game was on a beautifully warm, sunny afternoon in June 1967. My brothers and I and a bunch of our friends were slashing away at an old tennis ball, worn thin over countless hours. Dad emerged from the garage, already armed with one of his trusty old Northlands. He didn't stop to ask which team he should join. He chose to be his own team, and gave himself license to steal the ball from anyone, set up anyone, shoot on either goalie, or break up any attack.

Wading into the foray, he began by immediately pickpocketing the ball from our neighbor Scott Boyd's stick, then created a ten-foot swath of breathing room with his huge keister and elbows. He stickhandled through everyone, then threaded the ball over to Marty, who one-timed it past my friend Cole (who'd made the mistake of volunteering to play net before my brothers and Dad joined the game). Cole was lucky the ball whizzed past him; it would have hurt a lot.

Dad scooped the ball from behind Cole, stickhandled through nearly everyone again, then dipsy-doodled Mark, who was playing goal at the other end, until he was flopping around on the cement, helpless to defend the net. Then Dad passed it to me, and I banged the ball across the goal line. Dad played with us for another ten minutes or so, until he made sure he had done something memorable to every kid who was playing. "Memorable" as in trip him, whack the stick out of his hands, do a face wash with his giant palm, or grab his jersey/T-shirt. Miraculously he never hurt anyone. It was like wrestling with a tame bear, if there is such a thing.

In the last years of Dad's life I discovered that he still played driveway hockey just the same way. After his remarkable recovery from his stroke in 2014, he showed no mercy against his nine-year-old great-grandson, Brenden, who loved every high-sticking minute of it.

In any event, I can say with confidence that it was nearly impossible to steal the puck from Mr. Hockey. If I did get lucky enough to scoop it off his stick, he'd have it back before I even had time to celebrate. If he didn't get it back right away, he'd trip me or hook me just enough to throw off my balance, and then he'd steal the puck back. Son or no son, nobody stole the puck from Gordie Howe.

———

Dad was unmistakable in how he conducted himself on the ice. He took his time out there, gliding along effortlessly while everyone else seemed to be in a mad dash for the puck. His poise and coolness were deceptive, of course. He was just waiting for his opportunity. Then he'd pick up steam with a few long, powerful strides, scoop up the puck, and leave his opponents behind like pylons.

His patience created countless breakaways. He didn't always score, but he scored a lot. As he descended upon the keeper, time seemed to stand still. He'd fake a shot and wait for the goalie to commit. If he stayed up, Dad fired the puck low, just inside the post. He released the puck so quickly with his wrist shot or snap shot that the goalie wouldn't see it until he looked behind him in the net. If the goalie went down, Mr. Hockey would fire the puck over his shoulder or, if his pads were open, through the five hole. If the shot didn't go in, Dad parked himself in front of the net to capitalize on the rebound, confident that the puck would bounce back right onto his stick, which it did a lot. Dad's goals always felt a little like fate. Who was going to stop him?

Of course, Dad also pursued vengeance with the same unhurried deliberateness with which he racked up goals. God help anyone who took a cheap shot at him or his teammates. If you got a clean hit on him, he'd congratulate you. But if he thought you'd crossed the line . . . well, payback was coming. As a rule, Mr. Hockey didn't get you back right away. He'd wait. And wait. He was content to wait years, in some cases. His target always knew it was coming. The anticipation was almost as bad as the hit.

Players who found themselves on the wrong side of Dad's patience wore wounds like badges of courage. Bobby Clarke accidentally tripped Dad the first time he played against him. Bobby figured something was coming, but he didn't know when. Sure enough, later that game he found himself flat on the ice with a huge welt on his chest, compliments of Mr. Hockey's stick blade.

In Phil Esposito's first game against Dad, they tangled as soon as the puck was dropped. Dad's stick cracked Phil across his upper lip, and they both cruised to the penalty box.

In the box, Phil turned to Dad and said, "And to think you used to be my %*&%$@& idol!"

Dad's response was one of the most feared in the game: "What'd you say?"

Through the ice pack and bloody towel against his face, Phil found the correct answer: "Oh, nothing, Mr. Howe. Nothing!"

In a rare matchup in the 1974–75 season, Dad's Houston Aeros faced off in Detroit against the Michigan Stags at Cobo

Arena. A young, feisty Frenchman (I believe it was Pierre Guité) hounded Dad, doing everything possible to ruffle his feathers.

Dad eventually had enough. When a skirmish broke out elsewhere on the ice, Dad looked for Guité. When he found him, he dropped him with a single gloved hand. The player didn't return to the game.

Dad was escorted to the penalty box. The announcer, who sat right next to the penalty box, began to say, "Houston Aeros penalty, two minutes for roughing, number nine—"

"THUD!"

To be funny Mr. Hockey had reached over the glass with his stick and playfully knocked over the microphone stand. The announcer broke out laughing as he fumbled to regain both his composure and the microphone. Then he shielded the microphone with his body so Dad couldn't sabotage him twice.

"Number nine . . . Gordie Howe!" he finally managed.

The crowd roared. Only Gordie Howe could receive such applause from the opposing fans after dispatching one of their own players.

———

Patience comes in handy when you're a hockey legend. There was no quick way for dad to navigate any public place. So he'd savor it instead. As a family, we learned to do the same. After each Wings home game, we'd all wait patiently for my dad to shower, dress, do his interviews with the press, and then sign autographs for his fans. This often went on past 11:00 p.m., and sometimes even beyond midnight. I didn't mind; it was so much fun to watch Dad work his magic.

Occasionally I stood next to him just to keep him company. Any time I did this, he'd sign the program and then hand it to me to sign, saying to the fan, "You want *his* autograph; he's going to be the really famous one!" I found this very embarrassing, because I hadn't done anything worthy of an autograph. But I didn't want to disappoint my dad, so I signed away. Thus, a lot of folks with programs autographed by Gordie Howe at the Olympia in the mid-sixties may also have a smaller, more scribbly autograph next to his that sort of looks like "Something, something, something Howe." Yep, that's my autograph.

When I was seven, Dad drove me to the Winter Wonderland rink for a game. The moment we hit the door, he was mobbed by fans. I watched the pandemonium for several minutes— Mr. Hockey strangling and elbowing as many kids as possible in between signing hats, jackets, sticks, and faces—before I finally informed him that I was headed for the locker room.

"I'll catch up with you!" he promised. Dad kept every promise he ever made, and this one was no exception. Within a few minutes, he appeared, likely having signed fifty-some more autographs. Then the dressing room fell silent, because even my teammates were in awe of him. So were the dads. Finally, someone cut the tension: "Hey, look—it's Bobby Hull in our dressing room!"

Mr. Hockey laughed along with everyone else, then graciously made his way around the room, tying everyone's skates (he could get them tighter than all the other dads) and signing more sticks, gloves, helmets, jerseys, and even someone's cast. There always seemed to be at least one kid in a cast on our team. It was hockey, after all.

Later that season, I played in a tournament in Welland, Ontario. Dad signed autographs nonstop during the game, as patiently as ever. He must have told some of the fans that I was his son, though, because soon kids started crowding around my bench asking for autographs from me. Not wanting to disappoint "my fans," I asked a teammate to take my shift so I had more time to sign. It's not easy to write "Best wishes, Murray Howe" over and over at that age. My coach finally sent the mob away, even though my team fared better when I was off the ice.

Dad's patient demeanor didn't rub off on me when I was a kid. When I was seven, he and I shot a Wheaties cereal commercial, just the two of us. General Mills flew us to New York City for the shoot, and the next day we found ourselves seated in a fake kitchen constructed just for us. The director said, "Just pretend you're talking to your dad like you normally do at breakfast."

I dutifully informed him, "But my dad doesn't usually eat breakfast with me. He makes beds while I'm eating breakfast."

"Well, just pretend, then!" the director suggested.

"But what do you want us to talk about?" I tried to clarify. I wanted to make sure we were doing this thing right.

"Anything! The microphone won't be on." Exasperated, the director raised his hands to the sky as if to say, "Why, oh why, did they have to pick *this* Howe kid?"

My dad said, "So, Murdock"—that was one of his nicknames for me, along with Muzz—"whaddya wanna talk about?"

"I dunno, Dad. I only know that there's no milk on my cereal! Who eats cereal without milk?!" I raised my hand, as if I were in school, and pointed out to the director that I had no milk.

"Could somebody *please* get this kid some milk for his cereal?" He again raised his hands to the sky, then placed them on his hips as he paced back and forth, trying hard not to seem impatient.

But when the gopher returned from the store, I saw that he had bought a pint of half and half, not milk. And it wasn't cold at all.

I raised my hand again. "Um, I don't think this is milk. I can't put *this* on my cereal! May I please have some milk? Any milk is fine," I added, trying not to seem difficult.

So they sent the gopher out again.

Finally the milk arrived and all seemed well . . . except there was *no sugar.* What self-respecting kid eats Wheaties without sugar? Did none of these guys eat cereal? So away the gopher went again, in search of sugar in New York City. The director had to leave the set, and I expect he went out to the curb to smoke an entire pack of cigarettes. But eventually, the sugar arrived, the milk was cold and had been poured onto the crispy flakes, and the cameras began to roll. The director was the happiest man on earth.

Believe it or not, the ad came out pretty well. It ended with a shot of me firing a puck into a hockey net and a box of Wheaties coming out the back of the goal while the announcer exclaimed, "Wheaties, breakfast of champions!"

I haven't eaten Wheaties since.

———

Dad was also remarkably patient at home. Never in his life did he raise a hand or threaten to hit any of the Howe kids. He didn't even have to raise his voice. All he had to do was say our names in a slightly deeper tone than usual, and that was that.

We stopped doing whatever it was we were doing. All the Howe kids knew that Dad could flatten us with one hand if he ever felt like it.

Although I was keenly aware of the power Dad possessed in his massive hands, I knew Dad was a softy when it came to his children. When I was around five years old, I *loved* sleeping between my parents in their bed. It was the most comforting place on Earth. Each night, I attempted to sneak into their room when the coast seemed clear. Dad would invariably wake up and send me packing. Mr. Hockey was an incredibly light sleeper, with the keenest sense of hearing of anyone I've ever met. The moment I set foot in their room—no creaking boards or anything—he'd whisper, in that slightly deeper tone, "Murray! Go back to your room!" How could he possibly know someone was there? And how did he know it was me and not Cathy? I'd retreat to my room for about five minutes, then try again. And again. This cat-and-mouse game continued for what seemed an eternity, until my dad surrendered. I'd crawl triumphantly up the middle of their king-size bed and bury myself beneath their covers. I slept soundly until morning.

———

Whenever my brothers harassed me, I always appealed to my parents for justice. When I complained to my mom, who knew what's what, she'd chide my brothers, reminding them that she wasn't afraid to use a little hockey stick on their behinds if necessary. Dad, on the other hand, was Switzerland. He'd tell me to "shrug it off" and wouldn't reprimand my brothers in the least. I think it was just the way he was raised.

If someone harassed you in Saskatoon, you kicked their arse. But there was no way I could kick my brothers' arses. They were twice my size. So naturally, they simply waited until Mom wasn't home, and *that's* when they hunted me down for some taunting.

After one of these episodes, I was especially ticked at my dad for not standing up for me. Mom, sensing my frustration, suggested that I write him a letter to express how I felt. That sounded like a good idea to me. So I wrote, in giant letters,

Dear Dad,

I do not like you.

Love, Murray

Mom helped me address the letter, stamp it, and mail it. I was about six at the time, and I remember the entire process. It seemed like mailing a letter took forever. It still feels that way, since the advent of email.

A week after I posted the angry-gram, I had totally forgotten about it. I came in through the garage door after school, reveling in a glorious spring day and whistling my cares away. But as soon as I stepped into the house, I saw my dad, parked in a chair in front of the door. I couldn't enter the house further without going through him first. He was not smiling. And even sitting down, he looked at that moment to be about the size of a Kodiak bear. Maybe a little bigger.

I couldn't for the life of me figure out why he was blocking my entrance. I searched his face for clues. Nothing but scars and an occasional blink.

"Hi, Dad," I said, smiling (I always smiled).

He didn't budge.

"What?" I asked, getting impatient. I was a hyperactive

six-year-old, I was hungry, and Mr. Hockey was sitting between me and that loaf of bread on the counter.

Finally he spoke. "I got a letter from you today," he said in as gruff a voice as he could feign.

A bolt of lightning seared the top of my skull. I suddenly remembered. *The letter.* Why, oh why, did I write that letter? I groaned to myself. Why did I listen to my mom?

I thought about playing possum or faking a seizure. But that wouldn't faze Dad. I knew he'd seen worse. So I feigned amnesia.

"What letter?" I inquired.

"*This* letter," he replied, waving it back and forth like a dead fish held by the tail.

I read the letter as slowly as I could, stalling for time.

"Ohhhhh, yes. *Now* I remember this letter! But don't you see? I don't *like* you, Dad—I *love* you!"

He broke into a big smile.

Phew! I thought to myself. I had just received a last-minute stay of execution. Having Gordie Howe disappointed in you even for a moment was like capital punishment.

———

Dad was an incredibly loving and patient father, and a tremendous role model for how a father should be at home. Each morning when Dad was home, he'd get up early with us to help us get ready for school and to assist Mom with any chores. There were very few jobs he wouldn't do. And everything he did, he did well and joyfully. He'd sweep, wipe, dust, do dishes, make beds, fold laundry, and help us get dressed. The only thing he didn't do was cook. I have no idea why that was. If you put him in a kitchen, he would empty the dishwasher, adjust the magnets on the fridge, reorganize the pots, and scrub the stuff off the stove. But he would never touch any item that required preparation, including removing it from a container and placing it on a plate or in a bowl. He seemed to be waiting for someone to give him permission to access the food, even though it was *his* kitchen.

The only exceptions were cookies and steak. If there were cookies in the kitchen, he would eat them. And he loved grilling a nice porterhouse steak. Gordie Howe could grill with the best of them. Maybe it was because the grill wasn't in the kitchen.

He'd make my bed while I ate breakfast, which, ironically, bothered me. He was trying to be nice, but my mom had agreed to pay me a hundred dollars if I made my bed every day for a year. That seemed like a fortune, but I'm sure my mom figured it was a safe bet and a great way to motivate me. I faithfully made my bed every morning when Dad was away, but when he returned, he threw me off by making it for me while I ate breakfast. I *should* have made my bed right away, but I felt I needed a full bowl of Cocoa Krispies first.

Dad never rushed, never stressed, and never seemed to worry. Or at least he didn't show it. He had an enviable calm about him. He seemed to be joyful, gracious, and at ease, no matter the circumstances. In Hartford, Dad had a thousand-foot driveway. When it snowed, you'd think he'd be on the phone with a plow company so he could head out for hockey practice. Oh, no. He'd shovel the whole damn thing. Six inches of snow. Times ten feet wide. Times a thousand feet. Then he'd go to practice. At fifty-two years of age.

When Dad stayed with us in his final years, he continued to astonish me with his tolerance for his unconventional son. One afternoon after I got home from work, I suggested we head out to Highland Meadows golf course and hunt for balls. It was hiking with a purpose. He got his coat, ball cap, and hiking shoes on, and waited for me at the door. And waited. And waited.

I'd gone upstairs to change out of my scrubs. But then I'd made the mistake of checking my email, and decided I needed to respond to "just one more" before I forgot. Twenty minutes later, he was still there at the door, patiently waiting. He didn't yell, "Where the hell are you, Muzz?!" When I got downstairs he didn't say, "Where were you?" He just gave me a hug and asked, "Do you need any help?"

We then walked to the course, which was just around the corner from our home. We hiked the fairways for an hour or two, making it a competition to see who could find more golf balls. My eyes wandered. Dad's eyes methodically scanned the spots he knew golfers were likely to shank balls. He found twice as many balls as I did that day, and almost every other time we visited the course.

Once we had as many balls as we could carry, about thirty in total, Mr. Hockey searched for someone to give them to. He chose the friendliest-looking foursome, walked up to them, and gave them the balls. "One of these might get you a hole in one," he said. He was serious. These weren't range balls. They were nice Titleists, Top Flites, Callaways—you name it. No cheap golfers there. The look on the men's faces when Gordie Howe presented them with two dozen pre-owned golf balls was priceless.

I alternated longer walking days with shorter ones, to allow Dad recovery time. On a short day we putted the practice green at Sylvania Country Club or went to the grocery store, the library, or the local hockey rink. He'd retired his golf clubs several years ago, when the arthritis in his wrists and shoulders made it difficult to swing a driver or an iron. But he still enjoyed putting, and he held his own on the practice green. He beat me and his bodyguard handily. It was beautiful watching him patiently take a few steps back with his putter dangling to read the green, line up his putt, then take a few practice strokes to estimate the torque needed. He'd be within a foot of the pin on every shot.

Many patients experience depression after a stroke. Not Dad. Though he regained the use of his right arm and leg after his stem cell treatment, it took a while for his coordination to return. He'd try unsuccessfully to skewer a grape with a fork right-handed. Then he'd smile and say, "Oh, the hell with it!" and he'd switch the fork to his left hand and nab it successfully. I told him he could just pick it up with his fingers, to which he replied, "Too easy."

When we took Dad to the local rink, he'd stand for an hour or two in the freezing arena watching the kids skate around, never complaining of the cold. One time, a coach halted his practice and instructed his players to skate over to where Dad stood. The coach then hopped off the ice, asked Dad to stand against the glass with the team behind him on the ice, and—voila—a team photo with Mr. Hockey! Dad then greeted the players one by one, clobbering them on the helmet with his oversize mitts as if to say, "Nice job out there!"

On one occasion, a coach was in the center of a hundred or so players and their parents, talking about the introductory program. Dad walked slowly to the center of the circle and stood close enough to the coach to whisper in his ear, but he said nothing. I wasn't sure what he was going to do. Elbow him? Down him with his left hook? But fortunately, Dad just stood there. The coach sensed a presence nearby, but he was so engrossed in his presentation that he had no idea who was standing next to him. The crowd loved this. Finally, the coach looked to his left, and was at a complete loss for words.

When he regained his composure, he said, "Well, this gentleman obviously needs no introduction. The greatest hockey player of all time, right here at Tam-O-Shanter!" The crowd gave him a warm ovation, then mobbed him for pictures. One of the boys in that group was named Gordie, after Dad. Dad was just as impressed as his young namesake. Even after two hours at the rink, Dad didn't say, "I'm tired, let's go." I had to make that call.

After we got home, Dad could barely keep his eyes open long enough to brush his teeth and get his pajamas on. He was out twenty seconds after his head hit the pillow. He said "Thank you, Muzz" and that was that.

5

Live Selflessly

"If you want a good workout, grab that shovel over there."

It's 5:00 a.m. Dawn is breaking over the horizon. Another day. How many times had I seen the sun come up with my father? He and I both enjoyed the solitude of the early morning. Sunrises reflected on the surface of an unnamed lake in Northern Ontario. Or off the snow as a dark winter's night yielded to morning as we headed for my 6:00 a.m. practice. Or off our own front yard rink in Lathrup, from our vantage point at the kitchen table, sharing a quiet breakfast of eggs, bacon, toast, and black coffee for Dad, a bottomless bowl of Cocoa Krispies for me. You could probably trace a life, and a relationship, just in sunrises.

Sunrise signals hope. A new beginning. This time, though, it comes without my father. But there is something about being alone tonight with my thoughts and my memories that has kept my father close.

I see, now more than ever, how precious every moment is. I know I'm lucky to have had a year of these moments, these small things that tell us who someone really is. Sitting here now, I laugh a little remembering something that happened just last fall. Dad and I were heading out to pick up some groceries. As we crossed the parking lot, he spotted a teenage employee struggling to push a train of grocery carts back into the store. Dad could never stand by and let someone struggle, so he made his way over to help. The boy didn't want to let an eighty-seven-year-old man do his job for him, so he not unreasonably refused to relinquish the carts. But there weren't many forces in the world that could get in the way of Mr. Hockey doing a good deed. He just stepped into the space between the carts and the teen. The beleaguered employee had no choice but to let go. Dad pushed the cart train into the store, while the young man followed close behind, trying to look in charge. Once we got inside, I told the young man who had been helping him. The boy was ecstatic, thanked my dad, and requested a selfie.

"Thank you, Mr. Hockey." How many times have I heard that? How many thousand times more had my father? If there was one virtue that he hoped to pass on to the next generation, and especially his own children, it was an attitude of selflessness. To be compassionate, considerate, and thoughtful in all circumstances. His own joy and sense of purpose came from serving everyone around him. He absorbed their happiness, multiplied it, and reflected it right back to them. He lived to create extraordinary moments for every person he met. I believe it was this magnificent humanity that made him so beloved, so unforgettable. It seems that the truest measure of greatness is how much impact you have on others.

On the ice, no one was more selfless. He was the most prized player not only because he could do it all, but because he made his teammates better. After each shift, Dad made it a point to elevate his fellow Red Wings. "Nice pass!" he'd offer, along with a tap of his stick on their rear end. Or, "Great hit! He'll be feeling that one tomorrow!" A compliment from Mr. Hockey got a lot of mileage.

In practice he'd offer tips to the rookies. Dad was such a student of the game that if he told you something, you knew it was important. After a practice in 1971, he showed Mickey Redmond how "the puck has eyes," meaning that a player should shoot from the vantage point of the puck, which sees the net from a different angle than the player does. He taught Wayne Gretzky the value of a powerful backhand shot, which offers the element of surprise when properly executed. At practice in Houston, he showed my brother Mark, then a rookie, the power harnessed in the forearm, firing one-armed wrist shots into all four corners of the net.

He'd also take care of the smaller players. If an opponent took a cheap shot at them, Dad made it a point to reciprocate. If an opponent scored, Dad was the first to circle back to his goalie to tap his pads and say something encouraging, like "No one could have stopped that one. We'll get it back." His goalies especially loved him because Mr. Hockey always focused on coming back to help defend his own net. If he had played more offensively and selfishly, he could have scored a lot more goals, but would've been less valuable to his team.

He also demonstrated the highest level of respect for his coaches and general manager, even when he disagreed with them. That set a positive tone for the entire team. Privately he might suggest that a coach try something different, but he'd never say that publicly. In the latter part of his career, coaches relied heavily on his leadership and insight. The late, great

Bill "Foxy" Dineen especially valued his input. Dad had many simple observations that seemed almost trivial, but game in and game out, the simple things could make the difference between hoisting the cup or staring at it from the losing bench. For example, Dad was a right-winger. He noticed that he received a lot more passes from his centerman if that player shot left, because he faced Dad. Right-handed centers had their back to Dad. He also pointed out to Foxy that the Aeros had a defenseman with a bad habit of dumping the puck into the opposing end and then yelling at my dad to go chase it. Dad said, "I just spent half a shift winning control of that puck. Why fire it down the ice to go chase it again?"

Another observation was that if the Aeros were up several goals near the end of the game, they should forget about pressing to score more, which could frustrate the other team and incite cheap shots. Instead, he suggested slowing everything down, maintaining puck possession, and allowing the clock to finish the game. Foxy's willingness to listen to his players was a big part of why the Houston Aeros collected back-to-back championships under his tutelage.

When I sat down to write my father's eulogy, I wanted to get down on paper all the ways in which he was exceptional. There will never be another Gordie Howe. But right now, I realize how much of what was good about him was also good about the world around him. A willingness to help others was something his whole family stood for. In fact, his entire generation had discovered in the Depression that few us of can get by without the help of others.

Similarly, my dad was hardly the only player in the NHL to stick up for a teammate or to put the interests of the group ahead of his own. That's what a teammate *is*. My father would have done just about anything for the guys who wore the same sweater as he did. And they would have done the same for him. Hockey players may lose a few teeth here and there, but there is no question that the game, on many levels, inspires the best in all of them, not just Gordie Howe.

Still, there is only one Mr. Hockey. His level of dedication to his fans was inspiring. Everyone who requested an autographed picture got one, free of charge. My parents purchased the photographs and postage with their own money. Dad spent hours upon hours each week signing the photos, while both Mom and Dad stamped and addressed the envelopes.

He'd receive dozens of autograph requests per week, and many of those included a long letter. He'd read every one of them. If the letter was particularly heartfelt, he'd include a note with the picture, answering the writer's questions or acknowledging his or her kindness. Often he'd receive requests to visit someone who was ill, or to make an appearance at a banquet or charity event.

When Mark was laid up at the University of Michigan's Mott Children's Hospital in 1970, after knee surgery for a torn meniscus, my parents spent hours at his bedside. The nurses asked Dad if he'd be willing to visit the other children on the ward—all thirty-five of them. According to my mom, Dad spent time with each of them, signing their casts, or other body parts, and showing them how he could pull his finger off and then reattach it. Dad had sustained so many injuries in his career, and overcome so many setbacks, that he knew just what kids like that needed to brighten their day—a warm smile and a good laugh.

Throughout his life, he did his best to honor as many requests as possible, trying to balance his responsibilities as a father and husband with his responsibilities as a hockey hero. Sometimes he'd bring Mom, one of the kids, or our entire family along with him to appearances. In 1966, when I was nearing my sixth birthday, Dad took all of us to Saskatoon for Gordie Howe Day. Our road trip to get there—packed like sardines into a woody station wagon—was almost as much fun as the parade itself. How the hell we managed to squeeze three adults (the third was my babysitter, Dave Agius, whose sole job was to keep me alive) and four kids into a station wagon for three thousand miles, I'll never know. The drive took several days, not only because we detoured to cool places like the hot springs in Banff, but also because there were no interstate highways anywhere near where we were heading back then. We passed the time by singing a never-ending medley of road tunes, including "99 Bottles of Beer on the Wall," "Oh, You Can't Get to Heaven," and of course the "Name Game" song. The lyrics are indelibly engraved in my hippocampus: "Oh, you can't get to heaven (group repeats), in Gordie's skates (group repeats). You'll skate right by (group repeats), those pearly gates (group repeats)." This is why car televisions were invented.

I vividly recall floating weightlessly in the bathlike hot springs in Banff, delighting in the beauty of the Canadian Rockies and undeterred by the "rotten egg" sulfur smell. We stayed at the Banff Springs Hotel—literally a castle from my six-year-old perspective—and visited the spectacular Bow Falls. And of course, everywhere we went, people stared at us and said, "Hey, it's Gordie Howe!" Instantly, they'd forget about the surrounding attraction. It was the highlight of everyone's vacation, including ours.

The celebration in S'toon was replete with marching bands, TV crews, and the mayor christening Gordie Howe Park and presenting my dad with the key to the city. My fondest memory of that trip was riding in the back of a convertible during the parade. Though I knew Dad was quite a hockey player, I was blown away by how excited everyone in his hometown was to see him. Thousands of people smiled and waved at us (well, at my dad, with me sitting next to him), and my family and I waved back for what seemed an eternity. I was beyond proud to say I was his son.

Yet even with all the hoopla, I still didn't view Mr. Hockey as a bona fide celebrity like Batman or Superman. I reasoned that he was only "famous" here because it was his hometown. Perhaps I viewed Dad that way because that's how he viewed himself: just a prairie boy fortunate enough to get paid for doing what he loved.

Everywhere we went, fans wanted to put Dad on a pedestal, but he would have felt more comfortable picking up trash around the pedestal. He was humble and self-effacing, and he was happiest when he could find something to do to keep himself busy in the background. I never knew a dad who was more helpful around the house. Or around anyone else's house. If he was at a party, you'd most likely find him in the kitchen rinsing off dishes or cleaning the sink. Servers at catered events always got a kick out of seeing Gordie Howe carry dishes back to the kitchen. No chore was beneath him. Almost every banquet he ever attended, he was the first one to begin breaking down tables and chairs at the end. He'd stay until everything was put away.

He loved serving others, and the more manual the labor the better. He wasn't content to watch the gas pump's digits spin around while filling up. As a teen, he'd worked as a gas station attendant in Saskatoon, and thus was an expert at cleaning windshields. So in Detroit, he's squeegee fellow patrons' windshields while they gassed up. People were astonished that a Good Samaritan was cleaning their windshields. When they recognized *who* the Good Samaritan was, they were doubly amazed.

Every snowfall made Dad's heart skip a beat. He'd shovel our driveway, which was a good 40 yards spanning two roads. Then of course he'd do our sidewalks, and then the neighbor's sidewalks and driveways. Time permitting he'd also clear the ice rink he built in our front yard.

Mr. Hockey lived not only to be helpful but also to be a teacher. He looked for every opportunity to pass on what he had learned. Greg Wolff, my parents' longtime friend and insurance agent, met with my parents for the first time around 1980, when my dad was in his early fifties. After listening to Mom and Greg discuss the merits of universal whole-life insurance policies, annuities, and retirement planning (as if my dad would someday retire!), Dad politely excused himself. He knew Mom could handle the details.

When the meeting ended, Mom escorted Greg out. They found Dad chopping wood next to the driveway. He said, "May I show you something, Greg?" Whenever Mr. Hockey wielded anything—a hockey stick, a shovel, a sledgehammer, or any tool of mass destruction—he loved instructing others in its use. On that day, he showed Greg proper log-splitting technique, and invited him to take a swing. Greg was strong—a college athlete and a fitness buff—and it wasn't his first time chopping wood. But he wasn't going to say no to a legend.

So Greg brought the axe down gamely on the log, but the blade barely creased the dense hardwood. Dad repositioned Greg's hands, then showed him *precisely* how to strike the log and follow through. Greg, now embarrassed, came down on the log with all his might, but again, the edge bounced off. At that point, Greg was praying that Dad wouldn't ask him to do it again.

Dad consoled him. "Yeah," he offered, "that is some pretty tough lumber." Then Mr. Hockey raised the axe overhead, then brought it down like a guillotine, slicing through the log as if it were butter. One-handed. Greg was speechless. "Well," he said finally, "I guess that's why you're Mr. Hockey!"

Dad's helpfulness was usually welcomed. But not always. Once, after he'd shoveled a neighbor's driveway, the man came out and said, "I didn't ask you to do that." Dad shoveled it all back. On another occasion, he opened the door for a woman. Offended, she said, "I can get it myself!" He quipped, "Oh, I'm sorry. I thought you were a lady."

He was attuned to everyone's needs, and he made it a point to place other people's needs ahead of his own. This is how both he and Mom wanted the Howe kids to be too. Nothing drove this point home more clearly than the events leading up to my seventh birthday party. A few weeks earlier, I'd confided in Mom that I had a problem. There was a bully who lived down the street—I'll call him Butch for the purposes of this story. He was about three years older than me and twice my size. Butch's idea of fun was to stop any kid who attempted to pass his house and beat the crap out of him. If you sped past on your bike, he'd hurl a basketball or a rock at you.

My alternatives were to bring my brothers with me for protection, pedal my bike a half mile out of my way to avoid Butch's house, or ride like the wind on the far sidewalk and hope he didn't see me. He seemed to spend his entire day in his driveway waiting for someone to assail.

When I told Mom my dilemma, I figured her solution would be to instruct my brothers to beat the stuffing out of him, or to call the sheriff. But instead she said, "Let's invite him to your birthday party."

I was sure she'd lost her marbles, so I re-explained the situation. "No, Mom, you don't understand. This is a kid who *likes* to beat up other kids."

But Mom was adamant. She believed Butch just needed a friend. My head was spinning. I had invited all my best friends (like eight of them) to my birthday party, but as soon as they found out that *Butch* was going to be there, they'd all cancel. It'd be me and Butch, alone at my birthday party. I could see it now. "Here's your present," he'd smirk, and then punch me in the face. "A knuckle sandwich!"

I filled out his invitation, every word feeling like a tooth extraction, then mailed it. And for the next two weeks, I dreaded my party. Despite my dread, the day eventually arrived. Mrs. Hockey had made the coolest birthday cake: a chocolate train with the names of the guests on the individual cars so kids wouldn't fight over which piece was theirs. "Butch" was written on the caboose.

I was admiring the cake when, out of the blue, Mom yelled

to me from the garage. "Murray," she called, "one of your guests is here!" Thirty minutes early.

Who would show up thirty minutes early? I hadn't even wet down and combed my crew cut yet.

"Coming, Mom," I shouted. I bounded out to the garage, hoping to see Kimmy (the ballerina), or my friends Mary, Mindy, or Cole. But no—standing there, much larger than life, was Butch.

But he looked *different.* Less frightening. Instead of a torn T-shirt, he was wearing a plaid dress shirt and bowtie, and his hair was coiffed "just so" with a little Brylcreem. Instead of scowling, he was smiling, which looked sort of weird on him. And instead of brandishing a knuckle sandwich, he was holding a big wrapped present.

"Hi, Murray! Happy birthday," he blurted out like a kid whose car had just won the pinewood derby. For the entire party, Butch was as friendly and well mannered as a young man could be. He talked nonstop, kept asking Mom how he could help, and went to the back of the line during any games or when food was being served.

It was an unforgettable moment for me, watching the faces of my friends when they saw Butch at the party. Several whispered to me, "Why is *he* here?" But Butch was nice to everyone. He stayed another hour after the party to help clean up, and I wondered, "Is this really the same kid?"

After that, he called me virtually every day. We played together a few times, though it still felt unnatural, like dating a reformed psycho-killer. But from then on, whenever I rode past his house, Butch just waved to me instead of throwing rocks at my head. It was the most amazing transformation I have ever witnessed, even to this day. I'm forever indebted to my mom for teaching me the miraculous power of the Golden Rule.

———

Both Mom and Dad took great joy in giving a boost to anyone who needed it.

Several years ago a young hockey player from Sylvania named Jeremy Bigelow suffered a devastating cervical spinal cord injury and was almost completely paralyzed from the neck down. Jeremy was a fighter, and he and his family and friends began a campaign to help underwrite the costs of his expensive rehabilitation. A fundraiser was organized at Tam-O-Shanter, our local ice rink in Sylvania, Ohio, and our family donated a Gordie Howe–signed stick for auction. The night of the fundraiser, Dad happened to be with us. I was whipped after working a double shift and wasn't planning to attend, but our daughter, Meaghan, wanted to go and asked Dad if he'd like to join her. He was 100 percent in.

I decided to tag along to help. He was of course mobbed by the hundreds of guests from the moment he entered the building. He told the organizers, "Put me to work so I can raise some money for you!" So they set up a makeshift photo booth where you could get your photo taken with Mr. Hockey for a small donation. He posed for photos for almost three hours.

Mom and Dad were tireless in lifting others up. They flew in from out of town each year for Grandparents Day, and of course Grandparents Day became Gordie Howe Day at our kids' school, with all the students, parents, and teachers lining up for pictures with Mr. and Mrs. Hockey. They'd both faithfully attend our kids' dance shows, hockey tournaments, soccer tournaments, graduations, and other landmark celebrations.

Dad also loved pitching in for ProMedica, my healthcare system, serving as honored guest at the grand opening of their Alzheimer's care center, Wildwood Orthopaedic Hospital, and Flower Hospital's physical rehabilitation center. Ironically, Mr. Hockey experienced the rehab center's cutting-edge care a short time after it opened, when his knees were replaced around 1995.

Incredibly, the fundraisers and appearances he did on my behalf or on behalf of our kids were only a small fraction of the appearances he made for all my siblings, their kids, and countless organizations, including Make-A-Wish, numerous children's hospitals, and the Alzheimer's Society. He also helped raise millions upon millions of dollars through golf, tennis, and hockey tournaments, including Wayne Gretzky's annual charity tournament and the Hollywood Stars hockey games.

Mom was the catalyst for much of Dad's charity work; she knew what made him happy, and she knew how much good he could accomplish. She was also instrumental in organizing an unforgettable 1971 March of Dimes fundraiser game that pitted my dad, Uncle Vern, my brothers, and the Junior Wings against the Red Wings. Even I played, firing the game-winner past Wings goalie Jimmy Rutherford. He did his best to allow my limp wrist shot to trickle through his pads. Staged or not, it was one of the biggest thrills of my life. (That's the night the photo that serves as the cover for this book was taken. Funny how every good deed finds its way back to you, in spades.)

Another memorable moment happened in a charity game at the Plymouth Whalers arena in the Metro Detroit area in the early nineties. I was playing for the Wings alumni against a team of Plymouth firefighters or police officers or some other keepers of public safety. I noticed that the other club had a huge player on their roster. He wasn't a strong skater, but he was a beast. Unfortunately, I ran into him as I was carrying the puck with my head down.

These games were "no checking" by tradition, but of course in hockey, anything can, and will, happen. My head collided with his hip. He went flying. I stayed put. But I felt like I had just checked a sequoia tree. The referee blew the whistle and pointed at *him*, signaling a penalty even though I was equally at fault. The announcer said, "Plymouth penalty, two minutes for roughing and unnecessary falling, number 23, Kirk Gibson!"

"Ha, that's so funny!" I said to the Wings player next to me as I realigned my battered jaw. "The announcer just called that guy Kirk Gibson. I'm sure he gets ribbed a lot, because he *does* sort of look like Kirk Gibson."

My linemate gave me an odd look. "That's because he *is* Kirk Gibson!" he explained. As in, the 1984 World Series champion Detroit Tigers homerun hero. The firefighter apparently signed him to a one-game, no-cut contract, unbeknownst to me.

After the game I ran into Kirk in the hallway (again) and apologized, but he just laughed and said that was the best hit anyone ever put on him. He was very gracious and, as it turned out, a big fan of Dad's.

In the 2014 Scotiabank Hockey for Alzheimer's tournament in Vancouver, British Columbia, I had the privilege of skating in the equally expansive shadows of such iconic NHL alumni as Tiger Williams, Mark Napier, Mike Krushelnyski, and Marty McSorley, to name a few. I was especially careful not to collide with any of them.

When I meet hockey players I never cease to be blown away by their benevolence. Be it NHLers or weekend warriors. One who especially impressed me was none other than legendary Hollywood producer Jerry Bruckheimer. Colleen and I, along with two of our sons (Corey and Sean), had the privilege of meeting Bruckheimer at his studio in Santa Monica, California, in the spring of 2014. He was as warm and unassuming as Mr. Hockey. But what I enjoyed the most was seeing how much he loved hockey. Although he's in his seventies, he looks and acts fifty and still plays pickup hockey twice a week with distinguished linemates like Wayne Gretzky and Cuba Gooding Jr. Jerry and his wife, Linda, are incredibly philanthropic and remarkably down to earth. That's hockey players for you.

Another memorable hockey buff is Canadian actor and comedian Mike Myers. He told me a funny story that happened in the early 1990's at the Wayne Gretzky Charity Tournament in Brantford, Ontario. Mike and his then girlfriend, Robin Ruzan, shared a limo ride with my parents. Everyone at the tournament had been mobbing Mr. Hockey, including all the other celebrities. He seemed to be the "celeb's celeb." Robin was intrigued by my dad's extraordinary popularity. After a few minutes of light conversation, she could no longer contain her curiosity.

"So, Mr. Howe, what do *you* do?" she asked earnestly.

Mike's jaw dropped. Was he dating the only person in Canada who didn't know who Gordie Howe was? Mr. Hockey came to his rescue.

"I'm a professional caddy," he said, winking at Mike.

"Oh," Robin smiled, satisfied.

Mr. Hockey always left everyone satisfied.

Dad would do anything for anyone, but he was especially partial to young hockey players. In spring 2016, a peewee player who lived nearby asked if he could have an autograph. Dad signed a picture, and I called the boy's father to let him know he could pick it up anytime. The pair stopped by in the later evening, after I had taken Dad on a long walk plus some grocery shopping. He'd just eaten dinner and could barely keep his eyes open.

I hesitated to tell the boy that my dad was there and awake, because he was in no shape to do anything but sleep. But I thought it wouldn't hurt to ask. So I told Dad that there was a boy at the door who wanted to meet him.

His face changed instantly. He sat upright and smiled. "Well, bring him in so I can meet him!" he instructed. I invited the young hockey player and his father in to meet Dad. They talked for several minutes, with Dad employing vocabulary he hadn't used in years. He was explaining to the boy how to shoot and pass the puck, and the boy was mesmerized.

I jokingly suggested that Dad show him what he was talking about in the hockey room in the basement. This was an unfinished space where Dad and I played hockey with a tennis ball. I figured he'd be too tired even to make it down the stairs. I was wrong. "Hell, let's go!" he responded.

Dad passed the puck around with the boy for a few minutes, and then he said, "I'll shoot on you." The young player became a goalie, and Dad lit him up, ripping shots through the five hole and picking the corners, high and low. He had the boy in stitches. After about an hour, the kid finally went home—with an incredible story to tell. Dad went to bed and slept sixteen hours straight.

Dad was also the king of chivalry. Even in his last years, after his stroke, he raced to the aid of women to help them unload their grocery carts. He spit-shined his caregivers' cars. The last year of his life, when his endurance waned, he'd still sweep the back patio, if only for a few minutes. Then he'd hand the broom to me and say, "It's your turn." I got the message.

6

Be Humble

"Don't read your own press clippings. You'll start to believe them."

It's a little past 6:00 a.m., and Colleen is stirring. She'll be up soon. She's an early riser, especially when there are guests in the house. She'll want to make sure that the coffee is brewing, and that she's up to greet the neighbors when they drop off breakfast around eight. I assured her last night that I'd be up and would make the coffee, but she wasn't buying it. She couldn't sleep comfortably knowing that her husband, the only guy in the house who doesn't drink coffee, was in charge of brewing it.

I'm incredibly fortunate to have married such an extraordinary woman. She is constantly focused on the needs of others, and is as dependable as dawn and dusk. She has a keen sense of humor, is incredibly creative and bright, and she's infinitely loyal. To top it all off, she possesses a timeless, irresistible, Irish look about her, that never ceases to take my breath away.

Dad loved Colleen almost as much as I do. And he knew she adored him too; he could sense it. I woke up one gorgeous Saturday morning in July 2015 to find him sitting at the kitchen table, a feast of bacon, toast, oatmeal, an omelet, a bran muffin, and cup of Joe placed before him by Colleen. She was listening intently, his voice barely above a whisper, as he related a story from long ago, pointing to a photograph from one of the many books written by or about Dad or my family that Colleen had pulled from the shelf. This moment was important to him.

He finished the story with a chuckle, shrugging his shoulders as if to say, "Who the hell would have imagined that?" And Colleen chuckled right along with him. Then she rubbed his rock-hard shoulder muscles, and he pretended to fall asleep and plummet forward into his oatmeal. "Okay, Mr. Hockey," she said. "It's time to eat your breakfast before it gets cold. I'll finish that back rub later." Dad pushed his chair back, stood up, and gave her a long priceless hug, said, "Thank you," then sat back down to annihilate his feast. Colleen was a constant source of comfort for my dad; he knew he was loved. For that, I'm forever grateful.

It's difficult to fathom that I won't be able to listen to his soft voice, catch his impish grin, or experience his bear-sized hand crushing mine just to be funny. The moment I greeted him each day, he offered either a hug or a handshake, depending on his mood. If he was really relaxed, it was a hug. If he was still trying to figure out where the hell he was, it'd be a handshake. The moment he felt the smallness of my hand, and sensed my playful disposition, he knew I was the perfect candidate for a bone-crushing metacarpal squeeze. Which would lead to a good laugh. A great start to a great day.

When I was a boy, Dad wasn't too comfortable with hugs. Men didn't hug other men very often in Saskatoon in the thirties. So as a young father, Dad hugged Mom and Cathy, but Marty, Mark, and I mostly received handshakes. It never bothered me, because I didn't know anything different.

This changed when I was in high school. I had a friend, Mark Wensley, whose father hugged him all the time. Because of the esteem I had for Dad, I never felt resentful that he wasn't a hugger, or that he was gone a lot during the hockey season. It's just how he was raised, and what his job demanded. I still felt like the luckiest son alive. But I admired the kind of physical closeness Mark had with his father, and I wanted that with mine.

I knew that if I wanted to hug my father, I'd have to make the first move. And I saw my opportunity when I said good-bye to my parents before leaving for my freshman year at the University of Michigan. When Dad extended his big mitt out for a handshake, I instead surprised him with a huge hug.

It was weird for both of us. Holding me upside down by the ankles, putting me on his shoulders, pinching my arm with his toes—none of that seemed weird. But a hug between a father and his son, that was unusual. I liked it. A lot. So every time I greeted him or said goodbye to him from then on, he got a hug, whether he liked it or not. A handshake might precede or follow the hug, but the hug was going to happen.

I watched each of my brothers undergo the same metamorphosis in their interactions with Dad in his later years. At some point, we all realized that he wouldn't be around forever, and we decided to hold on to him as tightly as possible. It was a beautiful sight to see my tough-as-nails brothers embrace my tougher-than-nails father.

Over time, I believe Dad felt emancipated from his stoic upbringing, and evolved into an irrepressible hugger. Especially with women and children, including his own. Often when people extended their hand for a shake, Dad ignored it and went straight for the bear hug. When he hugged you, it wasn't a small "tap, tap, tap" on the back or an awkward bro-hug. It was a full-on squeeze-your-ribs-and-spine-until-something-cracked embrace.

I loved this closeness with Dad. I had always longed for a more intimate relationship with him. The older he got, the more he needed me, and the closer we became. Still, I never imagined there would come a day I'd be showering with my dad to help him reach where he no longer could and to keep him from slipping. Nothing brings you closer than that.

After Mr. Hockey moved in with us in the summer of 2015, he and I walked each day. I learned to stand about two feet ahead and to his right, so that if he stumbled on a crack in the sidewalk or a root on a trail, I was right there for him. I caught him almost every time. But on one outing at Wildwood Metropark, Dad, his bodyguard Pedro, and I wandered into some soft, deep sand. I was scanning the ground for roots when we happened upon a group of runners gathered after a jog. They recognized Dad and called out, "Mr. Hockey!" He made a beeline toward their huddle and managed to find a giant root protruding from the sand. He was down in an instant. He rolled and then leapt back to his feet before he could say, "Sonofabich!"

The runners looked concerned, but Dad was unscathed, save for a few patches of sand stuck to his forehead, knee, elbow, hand, and hip. He was still smiling, which was all I needed to know. The joggers, Pedro, and I all helped brush him off, and one of the runners asked, "Are you sure you're okay?" Dad laughed and said, "Aw, hell, I've been hit a lot harder than that before!"

That was true, but Dad's assessment of his injuries was not something I'd bank on. His indifference to pain was extraordinary. Over his career, he had hundreds of stitches sewn into his face without lidocaine. Even the everyday bumps and bruises of an NHL player would feel like the end of the world for most of us. Yet my father wore his battle scars like a badge of courage for parts of five decades. He'd never yield to pain.

That made him tough, but it also made him humble. Dad was the king of understating his own injuries. The king of understating *himself.* He had always emphasized to all of us kids that we shouldn't think too much of ourselves, be too proud, or elevate ourselves or our needs above others'. The bigger we thought we were, the more we set ourselves up for a fall.

———

Because Mr. Hockey was so humble, his transition to senescence was graceful and dignified. Time cuts down the proud, but Dad couldn't be cut down that way. Though his hair thinned, his muscles stiffened, and his memory faded, he was able to laugh it off. He'd look in the mirror before shaving and showering in the morning and he'd quip, "Aw sh*t!" As a physician, I've seen patients grow irritable and difficult as they sense their powers slipping away. Old age can make people angry. But not Dad. He remained patient, positive, modest, and pretty damn funny until the end.

I had admired his humility for as long as I can remember. It was a mark of self-confidence which allowed him to be aware of others' gifts. And other's needs. On the ice, he just did his job and that was that. He barely celebrated after a goal. He seemed embarrassed to raise his stick. He celebrated more when his teammates scored than he did for his own goals. And remember, Dad scored 975 regular-season goals as a pro. No one has ever scored more. No one ever will. Another kind of person might think that made him a pretty big deal. Not Dad.

Most sons grow up believing their father is the best. That's the way it's supposed to be, and I know now that it's one of the greatest things about being both a son and a father. No amount of fame or fortune is better than that. I wouldn't have adored my father any less if he wasn't the best player in the game, or even if he hadn't played hockey at all. I would have thought he was the best father in the world no matter what he did for a living. Yet I'm still in awe at the thought that *Gordie Howe was my father.* When I was a kid I asked him once how it felt to be the greatest hockey player on earth. He laughed out loud and said, "Oh, is that what I am?" Then he added, "You know you're only as great as your next game."

For his entire career, Dad lived in mortal fear that he'd be cut from the team during tryouts. Even when he was the league's MVP. That's why he considered his teammates adversaries until training camp was over. God help anyone who stole the puck from him, or got in his way, or happened to be a right-winger. After camp, he was the best teammate you ever had.

Just listening to him talk, you'd never imagine he was such a dominant athlete (until you happened to look at his massive hands and titanic shoulders). Once I watched a fan come over for an autograph. After my dad obliged, an old woman approached and asked, "I saw you signing something for that man over there. Are you someone famous?"

Dad didn't even blink. "No, ma'am," he replied. "I just used to babysit him."

Mr. Hockey was the definition of humble. When I was in third grade, my teacher passed out the latest edition of *My Weekly Reader*. This magazine typically had lots of cool articles about volcanoes and what kind of cereal astronauts ate and other important stuff like that. But this issue had a picture of my dad, along with a big article. Several classmates came up to me and said, "Wow, your dad's in the *Weekly Reader*! He must be really famous!"

The article had way too many words for me to actually read it, so I took it home to show my mom. "Hey, look!" I said. "Dad's in *My Weekly Reader*! Is he famous?"

My mom just laughed and said, "I don't know. You'll have to ask him."

My dad was on a road trip at the time, so I had to wait a few days. But when he returned, I showed him the magazine. "Dad, look at this! You're in my school newspaper, and it goes all over the country! Are you famous?"

He laughed and said, "Naw, they must not have had anything else to write about!"

When I was thirteen, I showed him an article calling me "the next up-and-coming Howe." I had cut the story out and was going to pin it to my bulletin board. Dad barely glanced at the paper and then said, "Murray, don't ever read your own press clippings. You'll start to believe them."

Dad was more proud of the fish mounted on the walls of our home than he was of any of his on-ice achievements. Mom displayed Dad's trophies in the family room and in their office, but Mr. Hockey ignored them. I, on the other hand, spent hours admiring them and wondering what it would be like to accept each award, wave to the crowd, and make an acceptance speech.

I found a few of his pieces of hardware to be particularly intriguing, including a huge trophy from Vic Tanny, the health club pioneer. At the age of thirty-six, Dad was named the world's most perfectly built man—without ever touching a weight in his life. Few people who'd seen him shirtless in his heyday would argue.

His quads were literally tree trunks, twice the girth of mine, and he had the biggest glutes I have ever seen. They must have weighed a good fifty pounds apiece. That's where all that skating power came from. Although he stood six feet tall, he had only a twenty-nine-inch inseam—shorter than mine. In other words, his trunk was colossal like a gorilla's. That's why running into him was like running into a motor home.

His shoulders were unlike those of any other human being. His upper trapezius muscles looked like NFL footballs glued onto either side of his neck, and they angled down sharply towards his upper arms, making the distance from his neck to his hands several inches longer than it was for most other human beings. This afforded him an exaggerated, simian-like reach. Much of his incredible upper-body power came from this unique physiology.

One of the noteworthy features of his body were his elbows, particularly his left, which looked like something out of a Stephen King movie. There was a glob of meat that jutted out about six inches from the funny bone (a medical term used by highly specialized musculoskeletal radiologists like me), and beneath this flesh, there was a jagged spike of bone, like a stiletto hidden by a sheath. This anatomical marvel was created by years of smashing his olecranon bone into players' faces, the boards, the glass, and the ice. Each fracture deposited a little more bone, like a stalagmite forming over time, until the present freak-of-nature bone spike had formed. It had been drained, resected, and sawed off at various times, but it just kept coming back.

Like his elbows, his wrists could take a radiologist's breath away. They were twice the normal size. This is because the bones had been fractured so many times that a thick rind of tissue had formed around them, along with a lot of fluid. On X-ray, Dad's wrists were so fragmented that it's difficult to pick out individual bones. When I show his X-ray to radiologists without sharing any medical history, they conclude the patient must have a "neuropathic joint," which means the nerves have been so damaged that the patient cannot feel any pain. This degree of destruction is typically only seen in patients with leprosy, severe diabetes, or other severe nervous system disorders.

One of Mr. Hockey's most astonishing feats is that he came out of retirement *with wrists like that*, was the WHA's MVP his first year back, and then played *six more seasons*. I can't imagine how much that must have hurt. But he had an amazing ability to defy pain. He was hard-pressed even to acknowledge its existence. He would've rather died than talk about his aches and pains—except when it came to his artificial knees, which he proudly flexed to demonstrate how they clicked and clunked when he moved.

Mr. Hockey's hands were the largest I have ever seen. At a party in Vegas many years ago, he was introduced to a super-model. He shook her hand as delicately as he could, afraid he might crush it; she instantly blushed and said, "Wow, I sure am glad you're not my gynecologist!"

He was quite embarrassed, but without missing a beat, he gave her a big hug and said, "Well, *I'm* not glad!"

His hands were not only huge but also astonishingly power-ful. Even into his mid-eighties, he could bring a man to his knees with a handshake. He could still grab your thigh and apply his viselike grip until you begged for mercy. Dad's unrivaled upper-extremity power, coupled with his superior agility, quickness, and fearlessness, helped explain how he reigned as the NHL's undisputed bare-knuckle, stick-wielding heavyweight champion for thirty-two seasons. Without a helmet. The legendary heavy-weight boxer Rocky Marciano once shook hands with my father and, without hesitation, remarked, "If you were a boxer, you would have been the champ." I know of no one who bested Mr. Hockey during his career. This feat is almost incomprehensible when you consider that not one NHL player today can retain the heavyweight crown for even an entire season. The toll on a play-er's body—not to mention his brain—is just too much.

Dad seemed embarrassed by the Vic Tanny award. He never spent a moment admiring his physique, and he laughed whenever he saw a guy posing in a mirror. Good thing I kept my door closed as a teenager.

Another trophy I loved was his Lester Patrick Award. I never knew what it symbolized, but the figure on it looked like an army general pointing directions to his troops. So I kept him in my room to participate in numerous skirmishes with my collection of GI Joes and little plastic army men. When Mom discovered what I was doing, she put General Patrick back in the office, although I doubt Dad would have minded. Only recently did I learn that the Lester Patrick Award recognizes someone who's contributed significantly to the growth of hockey in the United States. I consider it to be one of Mr. Hockey's most honorable commendations. In 2016, my brother Mark received the same distinction. That to my mind is an even bigger accomplishment for my parents. There's no greater gift to the world than to inspire the next generation.

———

Mom also taught me a lot about humility. For starters, she made sure that we kids understood what humble circumstances she and my father were born into, and thus she expected us to treat all people well, rich or poor. In fact, she was a champion for women's rights, the underserved, the outcast, and all minorities. She detested establishments that excluded anyone.

Most of the players' wives sat together at home games at the Olympia, which came in handy whenever a player got injured (a frequent occurrence). They comforted and reassured each other, and kept an eye on the kids if a wife needed to join a husband being rushed to the hospital. Most kids sat with their moms, except for me. I would sit still for all of about three minutes before going exploring.

The players' wives really didn't have anywhere to go. They weren't allowed in the Olympia Room unless they were taken in by a member. The Olympia Room was an exclusive club reserved for VIPs and season ticket holders. None of the players could afford the membership dues. Wives also weren't allowed in the Alumni Room, which was reserved for retired players and their wives, although the current players were welcome.

My mom and her best friend, Edna Gadsby, decided to take up the class struggle against this chauvinists' stronghold. Aunt Edna was an alumnus wife at that point because Uncle Bill had retired and was coaching the Wings. She brought my mom to the Alumni Room as an invited guest. Everyone in the room glared at them, but no one said anything. Soon after that, Aunt Edna was approached by a "concerned member," who suggested that it was unacceptable for her to bring my mom into the room with her. Mrs. Howe would have to stand outside the door! This was in 1968, at the zenith of my dad's career as a Red Wing. (I don't believe my mom ever told my dad about the incident, probably for fear that he would have unhinged the Alumni Room door with his elbow.)

Aunt Edna was flabbergasted. She informed the "concerned member" that she would bring my mom into the Alumni Room whenever she wanted. And she did, the next game. Right on, Aunt Edna! Mom and Edna didn't so much care that *they* weren't welcome—it wasn't their scene anyway—but they both felt strongly that *all* the players' wives should be allowed in. The policy just wasn't right. Wherever they sensed injustice, my mom and Edna were ready to fight the good fight.

There was a bit of hubbub in the front office and locker room following their civil disobedience, but soon after the players' wives were welcomed into the Alumni Room.

My parents felt uncomfortable being anywhere that was exclusive or in any way elitist. If someone wasn't allowed somewhere, my parents didn't want to be there either. Mr. and Mrs. Hockey were more interested in people's character than their net worth. Like my dad, Mrs. Hockey felt it was a privilege to chat with all fans, not just the ones in the private boxes. And she would *genuinely* listen to their stories and make them feel like they were the most important people in the world at that moment.

After every game, Mom waited patiently outside the dressing room for my dad, along with about a thousand fans. She blended right in with the fans, police, paparazzi, stadium crew, and billions of kids running around. It was always a madhouse—a shark frenzy—with everyone jockeying for position for an interview, a photo, or a Gordie Howe autograph. Dad accommodated every fan, listened to every story, smiled for every photo, and blushed with every kiss on his cheek. This would go on for an hour or more, often beyond midnight. Mom didn't wear a name tag or expensive jewelry to bring attention to herself. She just leaned against the wall while Mr. Hockey played his part.

Part of understanding your parents comes from seeing them through other peoples' eyes. I knew my dad was pretty great, and it wasn't long before I realized that plenty of other people did too. But it was seeing how my father reacted to his fans' adulation that really showed me the kind of man he was. One night at the Olympia many years ago, Dad had finished signing hundreds of autographs after a game. It was past midnight, and the security crew was giving my dad the signal that it was time for them to lock the stadium up. There were still twenty or thirty people waiting to talk to him.

He looked at my mom, then at his remaining fans and said, "I am really sorry. But I have to go. I will see you at the next game."

He headed towards the door, but the crowd followed him outside. He signed a program or two while he was walking, and then said, "I'm sorry, that's the last one." When he reached our car, he opened my mom's door for her (as always), and all of us kids piled in. But just as he was about to open his own door, a little boy about my age raised his voice above the crowd. "I've been waiting for you ALL OF MY LIFE!"

My dad froze, halfway into his seat. He looked at my mom as if to say, "How could I drive away?"

He got out of the car, signed the boy's program, and talked with him for a minute. He then signed autographs for the remaining fans.

I realize now that *this* is what made Dad so great, and why his reputation has never faded. He showed every fan, every child, that he truly *cared*. He showed them that he believed in them. They were important. That they could be as great as him, someday, in their own way. Mom and Dad both embraced this philosophy. They tried to pass it on to each person they met, especially their own family.

Humility can be taught, by the way.

And if seeing my parents' humility with my own eyes wasn't enough, my mother had a memorable lesson in store for me one evening. When I was about ten, I was in a back hallway of the Olympia, playing "cup hockey" with a few kids I had met while roaming the darkest recesses of the stadium. Cup hockey was simple: we dug a paper beer cup out of the trash, crushed it, and kicked it around like a soccer ball.

That night, one of the boys claimed that he was Bobby Hull's son. He went on for several minutes about how much fun it was hanging out with the Blackhawks, etc., etc. I called him out on it, telling him that I knew Bobby Hull very well, and this story was a crock.

The cup hockey game stopped and the boys listened to me describe how I had visited Bobby's family farm in Belleville, Ontario, and Bobby taught me how to milk a cow. I told them that he'd initiated me by squirting the udder's stream onto my burgundy penny loafers. Then I added, "I know you aren't Bobby Hull's son. But I *am* Gordie Howe's son!"

The kids burst out laughing, and one said, "Yeah, right, and I'm the King of England!"

"I'll prove it to you," I responded confidently. "I'll walk right up to Gordie Howe's wife, and she'll tell you herself." Everyone knew what Mrs. Howe looked like and where she sat.

The boys laughed again and said, "Yeah, right! We gotta see this!"

The gauntlet had been thrown.

I told them they each had to pay me a buck if Mrs. Howe affirmed my identity, and I would pay them each a buck if she didn't. I didn't have any money on me, but I knew it was a safe bet.

So all eyes were upon me during intermission as I strode confidently down the steps to the row where Mom sat. I simply said, "Mom, those boys over there don't believe I'm Gordie Howe's son. Go ahead and tell them."

My mom gave me a blank stare—she looked like a Stepford Mom—and said, "I'm sorry, who are you? Please step away from me before I call the police."

My jaw dropped to the floor. The kids, who were standing just within earshot, burst out laughing, and then ran away down the corridor to cherish this classic moment and replay it a thousand times in their minds.

———

I was listening to a program on NPR recently on the topic of dyslexia. The reporter said that as a result of the colossal challenges they face, dyslexic individuals are by and large hard-working, creative, patient, and tolerant. I immediately thought of my dad.

Dad was never diagnosed with dyslexia. But he failed third grade twice because he couldn't read. And although he did eventually learn to read and write, words were always a struggle for him. What I found so remarkable about Mr. Hockey was that he was the wisest man I've ever known, yet he never read a book in his life. Clearly wisdom is not necessarily something you read about.

I believe Dad always saw himself as the awkward, oversized Saskatoon third-grader who struggled to learn because no one knew there was such a thing as a learning disorder back then. The other kids just called you "doughhead" and made fun of you. It's no wonder Dad left school in the middle of grade eight and channeled all his frustration and humiliation into the one thing he excelled at: hockey. It became his safe harbor, his domain, and God help any boy who had to face him on the pond after mocking him in the classroom.

Despite his dyslexia, Dad was brilliant. He was much quicker in math than I was, and he loved working with numbers. He loved organizing and counting things wherever he went. He was a quick study at card games and board games, and he was a whiz at crossword puzzles. Dyslexics learn by memorizing whole words, and that meant his crossword lexicon was almost infinite. His spatial awareness and problem-solving abilities were a marvel; he could design a deck on paper in a few minutes and the final product would be perfect.

To my mind, Dad's academic struggles were his greatest gift. A prerequisite for the greatness of this invincible, humble hero. Because he was so nonjudgmental and accepting of others, he seemed able to bring out the best in everyone. He didn't care whether you were a physician or an electrician, a teacher, a pastor, an artist, a rock star, or a stay-at-home dad. He admired everyone's talents. Yet he envied no one. He never pined to be smarter, taller, thinner, or more musical. He was absolutely content with who he was. Growing up, I felt fortunate that both my parents loved and accepted me for who I was, and had no preconceived notions of what I should be. Their mantra was "Do what you love." Own who you are. Be grateful for the talents the Good Lord gave you. And never, ever forget where those talents came from. Mom and Dad never lost sight of those teachings themselves.

———

A few years back, the Kinsmen of Saskatoon, spirited champions for worthy causes in Dad's hometown, decided to honor Mr. Hockey at their annual Sports Celebrity Dinner slated for February, 2015. In the spring of 2014, they contacted my brother Marty, who normally handled the logistics of Dad's appearances. Marty told them there was "a snowball's chance in hell" of getting Mr. Hockey to the event. At that time, Dad was already suffering significant cognitive impairment, probably owing to a combination of traumatic brain injury and vascular dementia. In addition, severe spinal stenosis was catching up to him. It was a struggle for him to get out of the house, let alone travel to Saskatoon.

Marty asked Wayne Gretzky if he'd be willing to make an appearance in Dad's place; the rest of the Howe clan would be there as well, but without Mr. Hockey. Wayne immediately said yes and volunteered to donate his appearance fee back to the Howe Foundation. Planning for the event then commenced.

I believe the Good Lord is capable of throwing a curveball whenever he feels like it. But what happened next was a big one. By August 2014, Dad had gone downhill so far, and travelling had become so difficult for him, that our family decided it would be best for him to reside in one location for the balance of his days. (Prior to that, he'd spent two or three months at a time in each kid's home, which had worked great up until then.)

We decided that the best place for Dad was with my sister, Cathy, in Texas. Her husband, Bob, was retired, and he and Dad, who were great friends, could spend most of their days together, fishing, visiting with friends and Cathy's daughter's family, and enjoying the warmth and sunshine. In early September, I escorted Dad down to Texas, spent a week getting him settled, and then left him in Cathy's capable hands.

That's when the wheels flew off the wagon. On October 26, 2014, Dad suffered a hemorrhagic thalamic stroke. He was left with very little movement in his right arm and leg, and he could barely talk or eat.

My brothers and I flew down immediately to be with him. We brought in a team of doctors, nurses, and physical, occupational, and speech therapists. In addition, there was a massive outpouring of support from around the hockey world. Truckloads of mail, flowers, fruit baskets, candy, and other treats arrived, along with countless touching emails, tweets, Facebook posts, blog posts, TV commentaries, and news articles. Perhaps the most stirring for me was Keith Olbermann's ESPN tribute to Dad, which brought a rare smile to his face during his darkest days.

Hockey teams of all shapes and sizes also demonstrated their support. Our friend Drew Bradbury's Special Olympics floor hockey team in Grand Rapids dedicated a game to him. The Vancouver Giants presented me with a six-foot-long get-well card signed by most of their ten thousand fans. At the Red Wings game on Halloween night, fans were given "Get Well, Gordie" banners, and they initiated a pregame get-well chant ("Gordie! Gordie!") that brought Mr. Hockey to tears as he watched on television. I'd never seen a man so beloved.

Initially, Dad was stable but bedridden. Then, over the course of a few days in early November, he began to respond to his treatment, in a large part due to the outpouring of support and prayers. He just didn't want to disappoint his fans. He regained some ability to talk, and he was able to walk ten agonizing steps with the aid of a walker and my arm to support him.

But the stress and strain of being largely confined to a wheelchair and his bed created more physical difficulties for my dad. His back pain returned with a vengeance, and he required an epidural injection in mid-November. This treatment eliminated his pain, but he seemed to lose ground each day from then on. He soon became bedridden again, barely eating or speaking. As a family, we began making his funeral arrangements. His death seemed imminent.

Just as we began to accept what seemed like Dad's final bow, I received a call from Dave McGuigan, a native Detroiter who had worked closely with my mom and dad to promote youth hockey some years earlier. He was a huge fan of my parents. He worked for a San Diego stem cell biotech company and based on his experience, he was confident that their stem cells could help Mr. Hockey.

Because of the gravity of Dad's situation, as well as the paucity of data in the medical literature on stem cell therapy for stroke, I was beyond skeptical. But after learning more about it, the treatment appeared to be safe, and there seemed little to lose in trying. When I explained the situation to Dad, he gave me an immediate thumbs up. If his getting treated might someday help others, and if it might improve his quality of life down the home stretch, he was game. My family agreed.

Still, it would be like pulling the goalie with one second to go in the third period. With your two best players in the penalty box. A true Hail Mary pass. Not to mention that we had no idea how we would get two hundred pounds of dead weight onto an airplane from Lubbock to San Diego.

But on Sunday, December 1, when it seemed like things couldn't get any worse, they did. Mr. Hockey was unarousable, his face lifeless even when caregivers thumped on his chest. Fearing he had sustained another stroke, our family had him admitted to hospital in Lubbock. He was not eating, drinking, or responding to any stimuli. I emailed Dave and told him that as much as we wished to have him undergo the treatment, it looked like he would not be physically capable of surviving the trip. They wished us well and sent prayers our way.

Tests eventually confirmed dehydration rather than a second stroke, and Dad managed to open his eyes after treatment with IV fluids, but he still struggled to eat or communicate. He was discharged after three days, with a recommendation for a referral to a hospice. After he returned home, he was largely confined to his bed and unable to stand, but he was swallowing some food and mumbling a few words. Marty and Cathy were able to get him into a wheelchair for a short time, and he attempted to propel himself about the den using his good leg. Cathy and Marty called me and said, "It won't be easy, but we might still be able to get him to California."

Marty volunteered to be my wingman. We tried to locate a private jet to make it easier on Dad, but on such short notice that was a no-go. I booked us on connecting commercial flights, and Marty ended up being invaluable in hoisting this massive man into and out of the specialized skinny "aisle chair" that rolled him to his seat on the plane. Dad looked like Hannibal Lecter as he was wheeled aboard, strapped in with thick belts crisscrossing his chest and cinching down his arms and legs. He made the first flight without incident—until we landed. He was impatient to get out of his seat and tried to pull himself up even though he couldn't stand. With his left hand, he grabbed the tray that was latched to the seat in front of him and pulled it off its moorings. I was glad to see there was some fight left in him.

On the second leg of our journey, an angelic flight attendant took a shine to him and knelt in the aisle next to him for a good ten minutes, trying to understand what he was saying to her.

She finally got it: "I was a hockey player." I couldn't believe she was able to understand his whisper above the deafening drone of the plane. But her persistence and kindness were rewarded. Dad asked me for a pen and paper using hand gestures, and I obliged. He hadn't touched a pen in a month, and hadn't been able to sign more than a *G* even on his best day. He scribbled a bit, and lo and behold, a decipherable Gordie Howe autograph emerged—not pretty, but definitely his signature. Upon landing, the entire flight crew requested a photo with Mr. Hockey.

The next day, Dad underwent a baseline neuropsychological evaluation and a physical examination, and then I followed him into the surgical suite for the lumbar puncture. This was why we had come all this way. Everything depended on this ground-breaking procedure. I'd done my homework. So I took some comfort from the fact that my medical background allowed me to compassionately guide my dad through this intimidating, unfamiliar process comfortably.

The thing is, I knew it wasn't going to be easy. Because I'd taken care of Dad for so long, and because I'd seen his MRIs, I knew that his stenosis was going to be a challenge. Lumbar puncture is typically done at the lower lumbar spine, below the spinal cord, and where the canal is widest, L3-4 or L4-5. The needle is only about the thickness of a human hair, but Dad didn't have much canal left. It was going to be very, very tight. I could see that the doctor was looking where to go, and suggested he go higher up the spine than he normally would. He did, and the puncture went perfectly. He was grateful for the heads-up, and I was just thrilled that I could spare him and my dad some real frustration because I am a doctor myself.

Not surprisingly, Mr. Hockey tolerated the procedure nicely.

The neural stem cells were infused into his cerebral spinal fluid, and then he had to lie flat for eight hours to allow the cells to diffuse into his brain.

Dad wasn't too thrilled about lying down for eight hours straight, though. He cursed out Marty for leaning on him to keep him from thrashing around. I distracted him with an endless playlist of YouTube GoPro epic fails. At the end of his eight-hour incarceration, he said, clear as a bell, "I have to go to the bathroom," then he sat up as if he wanted to get out of bed. These were the first words I had heard him speak intelligibly in over a month. The fact that he sat up was equally flabbergasting.

I said, "Wait, Dad! You can't walk. Let me get the urinal."

He said, "The hell I can't!" and slid his legs over the side of the bed and planted his feet on the floor. I grabbed under his armpit to catch him, but he was bearing his own weight. Then he took a step forward. And another. If I hadn't been there, I wouldn't have believed it. He *walked*, with only modest assistance from me, the ten steps to the bathroom and back again. I was speechless.

He repeated this performance several times during the night. The next morning, he received IV mesenchymal stem cells. These were supposed to boost the effectiveness of the neural stem cells. After the treatment was done, Dad had a healthy glow about him.

The neuropsychologist tested him again before he left the hospital, and Dad was able to recognize 80 percent of the items shown. Before the procedure, he'd recognized less than 10 percent. He wanted to walk out of the clinic, but we insisted he use the chair so he didn't wear himself out.

Three days later, we flew back to Lubbock. But this time, Dad walked to his seat on the plane. Flight attendants who recognized him from his trip out were shocked. One looked at me and said, "Oh my god, is this the same man?" I nodded. When we reached Lubbock, I wheeled Dad to the curb, and then he got up out of his wheelchair, walked over to Cathy, and embraced her. She just lost it.

Within a few days, he was back to joyfully raking, sweeping, vacuuming, and doing the dishes. His physical therapists and speech therapists were astounded. Dad's recovery suggests that stem cell therapy holds great promise in the treatment of acute stroke and perhaps a host of neurologic conditions, but rigorous research is needed to confirm its safety and effectiveness.

My healthcare system, ProMedica, is working fervently to initiate a stem cell FDA-approved clinical trial for traumatic brain injury (TBI) as the centerpiece of a broad initiative (known as the Gordie Howe Initiative) to find treatment solutions for TBI.

Dad recovered so well that by mid-January 2015, he seemed very capable of making the trip to Saskatoon. We wanted him to experience one last time the love that would no doubt envelop him the moment he set foot in his hometown. Marty rung the Kinsmen event coordinator and said, "You're not going to believe this, but I think Mr. Hockey will attend. No promises, of course."

I volunteered to escort Dad to Saskatoon. On February 4, I flew from Detroit to Lubbock, then early the following morning Cathy drove back to the airport where a private jet would take us on an easy three-hour flight to S'toon. I was leery when the private jet showed up forty-five minutes late. I was even more leery when the craft turned out to be so small that Dad had to bend over ninety degrees to fit through the door and spelunk down the aisle. Shortly after takeoff, the pilot informed us that there were mechanical problems and we were diverting to Dallas. I prayed we didn't crash, but Dad was unfazed. Not his first rodeo.

In Dallas, we were told that repairs would take thirty minutes, and then we'd be off again. Five hours later, we were informed that the jet was broken, there was no other plane available and we'd have to spend the night. Dad had already missed the press conference by that point. I was not about to have him miss his entire homecoming.

"I don't think you understand the situation," I told the representative from the tiny airline. "This is Gordie Howe. He has an entire city waiting to honor him. I need your help in getting him there today."

The representative said, "I'll see what I can do."

I immediately got on my cell and asked the Kinsmen if they could work some magic. An hour later, we were on another jet—this one a little bigger. But the pilot cautioned: "I can get you two as far north as Minot, North Dakota. After that, I can't tell you what's going to happen."

I was flummoxed. But there was little else we could do but pray. We landed in Minot in blizzard conditions, and the pilot shouted back to us, "Good news! A jet from Saskatoon will be here shortly to get you home, Gordie!" Shortly thereafter, we boarded a beautifully appointed Kreos Aviation jet and were greeted by two friendly pilots with warm handshakes. "Gordie," they said, "it is an honor to fly you home to Saskatoon!" We downed a tray of sandwiches while the pilots fought through the whiteout conditions with smiles on their faces. Finally we landed in Saskatoon around 10 o'clock, two hours past Dad's typical bedtime, ending our thirteen-hour ordeal. The jet door opened, and Dad descended the steps to face a throng of reporters, microphones, and blinding TV camera lights—and a frosty minus 30 Celsius Saskatoon breeze.

—

And what a homecoming it was. The Kinsmen dinner is a feature of life in small towns across Canada. They happen all the time, and across the continent. But there will never be another like the one in Saskatoon in 2015.

Dad had been invited because the town was renaming the hockey rink in his honor. Just try to imagine it. One day, you're playing shinny under the bridge across the South Saskatchewan River, warming your hands between shifts over the fire in a rusty barrel. The years pass, and now there is a park and a rink with your name on them. This dinner is just for you. When you enter the room, fifteen hundred people chant your name. Some of the greatest players in the history of hockey are there to shake your hand. Because you inspired them. You made them better. The whole country is watching. "I think the people of Saskatchewan and the people of Canada want that one chance to thank him for what he's done," said Wayne Gretzky.

No daydream could ever be this complete. And yet, despite all that—all the honors, the toasts, the fame—nothing had changed Dad. Although he had only recently rebounded from his stroke, he wowed the crowd by chatting it up with fans and event staff, including the kitchen crew. The icing on the cake was when he climbed the stairway to the stage to accept a sign renaming the local rink Gordie Howe Kinsmen Arena. He remained on stage, and there was not a dry eye in the room as The Great One, the Hulls, Kelly Chase, and Mark and Marty shared stories of what Mr. Hockey meant to them.

A few of the stories shared that night still stand out in my mind. Bobby Hull described standing outside Maple Leaf Gardens in the sleet and the rain as a ten-year-old, hoping to get tickets when the Red Wings were in Toronto. He finally got inside, and was not disappointed. Mr. Hockey scored a big goal, and Hull reacted, "My dad looked at me and said, 'Robert, when you can shoot the puck like that, you can play in this league.'" The Golden Jet also remembered asking my dad for an autograph for his own father after the game. Bobby said that autograph was his father's most prized possession.

Gretzky recounted how his favorite Christmas gift was a Gordie Howe jersey. And he admitted that the only school project for which he'd ever received an "A" was a report on Mr. Hockey.

Dennis Hull, a truly gifted comedian, told the story of his first encounter with Gordie Howe, when he was a young member of the Chicago Blackhawks. He wasn't seeing much ice time, but he was so enthralled with Howe that he reached out and touched him with his gloves when Dad skated by. He did this once, twice, three times.

Then, in the third period, Billy Reay, Chicago's legendary coach, tapped Hull on the shoulder. "Go out and watch Howe," he said.

"I said, 'I can see him fine from here,'" Hull recalled.

At one point, Hull actually thought he might get a shot at a goal. But he soon realized his skates weren't touching the ice. Mr. Hockey had grabbed the back of Hull's pants and lifted him off the ice with one hand.

"He said, 'Where do you think you're going?' I said, 'Anywhere you want, sir.'"

After the ceremonies concluded, Dad spent a good hour making his way to the waiting limo. He posed for more pictures, and joked some more with Wayne, the Hulls, and our family. Eventually we retreated to our hotel room. It was close to 10:00 p.m. Before we went to sleep, Dad and I talked about all the kind words that were spoken about him. He joked, "Did I do all that?" I assured him he did. And more.

Despite Dad's remarkable humility, he was only human. Back in the late eighties, my brother-in-law, Wade, overheard him humming in the shower. The tune sounded familiar, and finally Wade recognized it. It was a catchy Canadian tune recorded in 1963 by Big Bob and the Dollars: "Gordie Howe Is the Greatest of 'Em All!"

7

Be Tough

"There's no such thing as cold weather. Only cold clothing."

It's almost 7:00 a.m. Colleen woke up a while ago. "Did you stay up all night?" she asked with a yawn.

"I think I did," I joked. "How'd you sleep?"

"Not bad, but too short," she said with another yawn.

I suggested she go back to sleep and let me take care of the breakfast and coffee.

"No, thanks. I've got way too much to do," she said, already heading for the bedroom door. Colleen is the most responsible human being I've ever met. She was going to make sure everything got taken care of today, including the obituary, the handout for the private visitation, the handout for the public viewing, the funeral details, the press release, and food for the twenty-some family members who were staying with us or our neighbours. I'd help, but Colleen would make sure it was done right. It's what engineers do. I was grateful for her efforts.

Even though my brain is craving a few hours of precious REM, I refuse to yield. There's so much I want to say in Dad's eulogy, so many stories to share. His impact was so immense, it seems impossible to pack it all into a single portrait. Superlatives aren't enough to describe him. It's the countless moments that barely register in memory that define him. Not big goals, but a quiet smile or even something he might have done when no one was watching.

A single moment can last a lifetime. William Clay Ford Jr., the executive chairman of Ford Motor Company and great-grandson of Henry Ford, recently was quoted as saying that one of his happiest childhood memories was attending the Howe–Gadsby Hockey School. Ford, then eight, wanted to show Dad—his hockey idol—his work ethic and toughness. He put his head down to skate hard. "The next thing I know, I was slammed," he recalled. "I've never been hit so hard in my life. I'm lying in this heap, and it's Gordie looking down at me. He says, 'Son, always skate with your head up.' I was so honored to have been checked by Gordie Howe. That was the coolest thing that ever happened to me."

Yes, Dad knew how to make a lasting impression. Of course, as his own son, it took me some time to realize how special he was. I vividly remember lying on our living room floor when I was about five. Whenever Dad had an away game, our family would gather around the TV to watch him play. I would set up my Hot Wheels while Cathy painted or read a magazine, Mom crocheted, and my brothers wrestled or played "little hockey" during intermissions. This was pretty much our routine for those away games. After a few years of this, I decided to buck convention.

"Mom, why do we always have to watch Dad on TV?" I asked. "Batman is on now, and right after that the Green Hornet."

"Don't you want to watch your father?" Mom said in surprise.

I thought about that for a moment. "But I see Dad all the time, and I hardly ever get to see Batman."

Mom laughed, then explained, "Well, honey, we want to watch your dad to cheer him on and to make sure he doesn't get hurt."

"Get hurt?" I countered. "The guys on the other team are the ones who should be worried about getting hurt. Dad can take care of himself."

Two minutes later, the play was whistled down. The players had piled up in front of the opposing team's net. Dad was on top of the pile, as expected. Slowly, all the players got up . . . except my dad.

"Gordie Howe seems to be hurt," the announcer observed. "He looks to be in a lot of pain."

The trainers rushed onto the ice and surrounded him.

"Oh my god," I thought. "I just made my dad get hurt! God is punishing me for wanting to change the channel!"

My mom knew what I was thinking, but she didn't rebuke me. She just got on the phone with the Red Wings and asked them to call her as soon as they knew what was going on.

It turned out that Dad had broken several ribs by falling directly onto the point of another player's skate blade. When he returned home, his rib cage was wrapped in a Velcro support vest.

"It only hurts when I laugh or breathe," he said. That made him laugh, of course, and he winced as if he had just chopped off his toe with an ax. That's right—I'm one of a tiny number of people on earth who have seen Gordie Howe wince. But the next night he was back on the ice again.

Mr. Hockey was as tough as they came. In large part, this came from his father, Albert. Dad described him as "one tough sonofabitch." Ab was a vicious brawler who fought in make-shift bouts held at neighboring farms. Huge hands. Fast. Fearless. All-in. Ab picked up quite a bit of cash at these bare-knuckle pummel-fests because he rarely lost a match. He also got into quite a few barroom brawls, including one where the local police tried to break things up and Ab inadvertently clocked a cop, resulting in a night in the local jail.

Grandpa Ab demanded toughness from his sons, especially young Gordon. He was the biggest, strongest kid around, and Ab knew it. One day, he asked the guys on the Ukrainian road crew he supervised to take note of a large boulder. It was huge—the better part of 250 pounds, according to my dad. "Ten bucks says my boy can hoist that rock onto that truck bed," he said. Ab got lots of takers. Ten dollars was a small fortune in Depression-ravaged Saskatoon. Then he called Dad over and ordered him to lift the rock onto the truck.

My dad looked at the massive boulder and knew there was no getting out of this. Better to be crushed by the boulder than to incur Ab's disapproval. So he did as he was told. Ab collected a lot of cash from his workers.

Brute strength doesn't always equate with toughness, but in Dad's case, he defined both. I ponder this thought while reclining on the bed, and it occurs to me that Dad's toughness was at least partly generational. You did what you needed to do to survive in Depression-era Saskatoon.

Dad used to tell me that when he was a kid, the house had no running water, so one of his jobs was to hike several blocks to the hand pump, fill two five-gallon buckets, and hoof them back. He did this most days, summer and winter. Naturally, he and his siblings tried to be as frugal with their water as possible, so they didn't have to make more trips than necessary. As my dad put it with a smile, "We didn't wash much back then."

Except for a stove in the kitchen, most of their homes had no heat. Before bed, each of the kids would warm a stone in the stove, then carry it with a blanket up to bed and toss it under the covers to keep them warm. Add in three or four thick quilts, a hat, socks, and a nightshirt, and they were toasty warm—at least until they had to get out of bed in the morning. Then they sprinted downstairs and huddled around the stove again. Most of the homes they lived in had only three bedrooms: one for the boys, another for the girls, and the third for Ab and Katy.

For most of his boyhood, Dad and his siblings slept on the bare floor or on pallets. No mattress or bed. As a teen, my dad and his brother Vic nabbed a bunch of mattresses tossed out of a Saskatoon hotel. They scattered those mattresses across the floor and, according to Dad, "slept wherever there was a spot." It is nothing short of incredible that so much changed in one generation. Dad went from huddling on the floor without a mattress to sleeping in cozy hotel rooms (albeit with a burley roommate who often snored up a storm).

No matter how cold it was, the kids spent most of the day outside, since there was no room or privacy inside. From the age of six, when Dad got his first pair of skates, he played hockey all day, every day. He skated on the roads and the deep ditches (called sloughs), in neighbors' backyards, and on the South Saskatchewan River beneath the Grand Trunk Bridge. A game was always under way, and many lasted until dark. Most of the players were older, bigger, and meaner. They knocked Dad down, tripped him, and whacked him with their sticks until he coughed up the puck. If you think you're tough, try playing an all-day outdoor hockey game against a bunch of kids much older than you. That's Canadian tough. If you had a broken nose or lost some teeth, you didn't cry. You just played harder.

To keep warm, the players erected a makeshift shack next to the river and started a fire in a fifty-gallon drum. Those who weren't on the ice thawed their feet and hands and stoked the fire. Every couple of minutes they'd make a shift change. That kept legs fresh and toes warmer. I'm sure there must have been a lot of frostbite back then. Saskatchewan kids just learned to ignore it. Even today, you'll find a makeshift rink outside every grade school in Saskatoon, including Dad's alma mater, King George. If school is out, a game will be on.

I asked my dad once how he could possibly have survived such brutal temperatures all day long. He said, "I wore about six layers of clothing—hats and scarves and sweaters and more sweaters, and a few more sweaters just in case. There's no such thing as cold weather, Murray. Only cold clothing."

———

When my dad was around seven, he began working his family's vegetable garden in the backyard. A couple years later, he was sent to work on his sister's forty-acre farm, eighteen miles out of town. He would ride his bike back and forth, sometimes staying at the farm for several days or weeks at a time. His brother-in-law Fred had Dad working from dawn to dusk. He drove the tractor, dug miles of fencepost holes, plowed the acreage, milked cows, bailed hay, and cleaned the stalls. The dirtier, harder, or more dangerous the job, the more likely Fred was to ask my dad to do it. The word "no" was not in Mr. Hockey's vocabulary.

One morning when Dad was about twelve, Fred handed him a rifle and said, "Go get the bull and bring him into the stall."

Dad looked at the gun and asked, "What's this for?"

Fred winked and said, "You might need it."

My dad had no idea what his uncle was talking about. But if someone hands you a gun and suggests you may need it, you're probably justified in worrying a bit. Still, Dad marched right out to that two-thousand-pound perpetually pissed-off animal and managed to get a rope around its neck. The bull allowed Dad to lead him close to the barn entrance. Then the beast changed his mind.

He tried to pin Dad against the door of one of the stalls. Dad managed to free up the rifle, and he shot the bull point-blank in the shoulder. That distracted him long enough for my dad to vault over the top of the stall to safety. As the bull kicked and rammed the walls of the stall, Dad sprinted for the barn door. "Take that, you &^$&$^&@ bull!" he shouted as he slammed the door closed, trapping the animal inside. Mission accomplished.

Dad escaped with only a few cuts and bruises. And for all you bull lovers out there, the bovine did not sustain any serious injuries in the telling of this story. The rifle wound was like a bee sting for the animal, and he healed up just fine—at least well enough to be able to mate several more times. But his ultimate destiny was to become rib-eye steaks for the Howe family. "Best steak I ever had!" my dad told me.

———

My brother Marty played alongside Dad in the WHA and the NHL, and he knows better than anyone how Mr. Hockey defined toughness on the ice. Marty is a big, strong guy. He can take care of himself. But he had an even tougher guy on his line for most of his career. "There are five things you didn't do to Gordie Howe," Marty says with a wry smile whenever the topic comes up. "Embarrass him, grab his stick, hook him, annoy him in any other way . . . or touch his kids."

Dad applied these rules to teammates, by the way. Brad Selwood, Dad's teammate on the Hartford Whalers, inadvertently grabbed Mr. Hockey's stick during practice in 1979. Dad instinctively jerked his elbow backward like a recoiling cannon, while yanking his stick and Brad forward. Mr. Selwood was out for quite a while, according to Marty. Serge Bernier, playing for the Quebec Nordiques, got a piece of Marty one night. Dad then hit Serge so hard that after struggling to stand he skated over to the wrong bench. The Aeros players told him to turn around and go the other way. The play continued as he painstakingly fumbled his way back to the correct bench for some much-needed medical attention. After the game, Dad undressed in the locker room next to teammate Morris Lukowich. Dad lamented, "I must be getting old."

"Why's that?" Morris inquired.

Dad replied, "In my heyday, guys didn't get up after I hit them hard."

Not even fans were immune from Dad's sense of rink justice. The arena that was home to the WHA's San Diego Mariners had chicken wire above the dasher boards instead of Plexiglas. There was a San Diego fan seated rinkside who thought it was funny to get his feet up and kick any Aeros player who was checked into the wire in front of him, usually in the head.

As Marty and Dad cruised into the face-off circle one game, Mr. Hockey gave Marty a wink and said, "Watch this." Marty knew that anytime Dad said those words, something epic was about to happen. Normally, Dad lined up in the "slot" for an offensive-zone face-off. This time, he set up on the hash marks by the boards. When the puck was dropped, Dad nabbed it but then passively allowed a defenseman to ride him into the corner boards right in front of the chicken-wire kicker. Before the fan could get his feet up, Dad shot the butt end of his stick through the mesh and into the guy's chest. Message delivered.

In a game against the WHA's Cleveland Crusaders, a heckler a few rows behind the Houston Aeros bench started hurling slurs at the Howe boys. "You guys suck!" The usual stuff. Dad and my brothers had learned to ignore drunken ignorance. But this time it got personal. The guy called Dad's recently deceased mother a whore. Dad was on the ice at the time and didn't hear it, but the Aeros coach, the late, great Bill Dineen, did.

Bill was just a rookie on the Wings when Mr. Hockey was in his prime, and he idolized Dad, as many other NHL players did. After Bill retired from playing, he became a coach and worked his way up through the ranks to lead the Houston Aeros. Although Mom planted the seed with Bill for the Aeros to draft Mark and Marty "underage" (after a chance meeting following the Memorial Cup championship in 1973) it was Bill's brilliance and fortitude that made it all happen. I still vividly recall standing in our kitchen in Detroit in 1973 when Bill called to inform my mom that he had the green light to draft Mark and Marty. I had no idea who he was, but it was clear that whatever he told Mom was about the best news she'd ever received.

And when she handed the phone to Dad, he got about as excited as I'd ever seen him get. It was during that conversation that dad humbly, almost apologetically, tested the waters with his old friend. "Well, what would you think if another Howe laced up the skates to join the boys?" For a moment I was hoping he was talking about me, but apparently the Aeros weren't interested in a twelve-year-old. Bill, however, was ecstatic at the prospect of coaching his forty-five-year-old hero, and making hockey history.

All that is to say, Bill was much more than a coach. He turned to Dad for coaching advice, and the two were friends outside the rink. Bill had also known my grandmother, and he understood what she'd meant to my father. He couldn't stand idly by while the drunk disparaged Katherine Howe. So he scaled the Plexiglas barrier behind the Houston bench and sprinted up the steps to teach the guy some manners. Unfortunately, the fan had many drunken friends who piled on Coach Dineen.

Dad didn't know any of this was happening until the whole crowd gasped and he turned toward the stands. He looked up and saw Bill getting gang-whooped. I can't imagine what the fans must have thought when they saw an angry Gordie Howe leap over the glass—skates, stick, and all—and wade into the crowd to reach his friend. He got Bill back on his feet and blocked for him until the coach was safely back on the bench. In the meantime, about half the Aeros had joined the scrum. The police poured in, the game was terminated, and that was that. While some might say Mr. Hockey's on-ice brutality crossed the line, I would argue that he was just being smart. In a sport as brutal as hockey, if you are king of the castle, every opponent is gunning for you. If you allow your adversaries to take liberties, your career will be short-lived.

When Dad came out of retirement at age forty-five, he had no intention of having his comeback shortened by some hungry young buck half his age. Mr. Hockey quickly received a new nickname: "Rookie-killer." Each time he'd face-off against a rookie, he'd notch his opponent's forehead with his stick blade. Not enough to knock the young man out, but just enough to draw a little blood. And send a message. The smart players left him alone.

He was ferocious for sure, but he could also endure the kind of damage that would make most men think about doing something else for a living. In Dad's second season with Houston, in 1974–75, he was pegged in the back of the head in a scrimmage by a wicked errant slap shot, compliments of his own defenseman, John Shella. Dad was out cold. He landed facedown with no helmet on the unforgiving ice. He regained consciousness after a minute or so. Then he stood up and, against the trainer's advice, finished the practice. Unbelievable.

Perhaps an even more amazing feat was when he went headfirst into the boards in 1950, suffering an acute intracranial bleed. He had to have a hole drilled in his head to relieve the pressure—while he was awake. (I've seen Dad's CAT scan and MRI images, and can attest that the hole was still there decades later.) He came back the next season and was league MVP. I'd say that's tough.

———

Pretty much nothing about my father was at the same scale as other people. So the thing that may be most amazing of all is that he was bullied as a child. Gordie Howe, perhaps the most bully-proof human ever to walk the face of the earth, was bullied.

There was no such thing as a learning disability back in the Depression. As far as teachers were concerned, there were smart students and backward students. Dad could lift a bag of cement under each arm with ease, but reading a page of a book took everything he had. He struggled in school, and the other kids saw their chance to pick on someone. They called him "doughhead" or "bonehead."

He channeled his frustration into his legendary ferocious-ness on the ice. Hockey was his outlet, his safe haven. I suf-fered from the opposite problem: I excelled academically, loved school, and consumed books like bowls of chocolate ice cream. But when it came to hockey, it took everything I had just to keep up. School was my outlet, hockey my Achilles' heel.

No one expected this of a Howe, least of all my brothers, who used to suggest that I was adopted. People who knew Marty and Mark and assumed I would turn out like them were disappointed when they saw me on the ice. But it worked the other way around in the classroom. I had moved to Toronto to play junior hockey, just as my brothers had done, and enrolled in a high school near theirs. Midway through my first Canadian class ever, I received a message to go down to the counselor's office immediately. I thought to myself, "What did I do?" Perhaps it was an immigration issue or I had broken the dress code with my torn hockey T-shirt.

As soon as I got to the office, the guidance counselor ripped into me. "If you think you are going to float through this school and graduate," he yelled, his veins popping out of his forehead and his face beet red, "you are sorely mistaken! I know your brothers, and I have my *eye on you*, so you'd better watch your p's and q's. Do you read me?" I assured him I read him loud and clear.

When I went home for lunch, I called my parents. "What did Mark and Marty do in Toronto to get into so much trouble?" I asked.

My mom laughed. "That was the problem. They didn't *do* anything. They didn't go to class!"

That explained a lot. After lunch, I returned to school and finished the day with physics. And guess who my teacher was? Yep, Mr. Phillips, the guidance counselor. He made me sit in the front of the class so he could "keep an eye on me," but I had a surprise for him. I was the kid shooting his hand in the air to answer every question. I couldn't help it. I loved this stuff, whether it was science, math, writing, or music. I loved just about every subject.

It took a while to convince Mr. Phillips I wasn't trying to trick him somehow. He clearly didn't trust anyone with my last name. But in time, I won him over to being one of my biggest supporters.

I loved going to school in Toronto, but playing junior hockey there was another story. I was fortunate to land on the same team as Wayne Gretzky, Paul Coffey, and a few other future NHL stars. That part was fun. There's nothing better than being on the ice with players who love the game—unselfish, creative hockey players who need nothing more than a puck and a stick to be happy. But getting crushed along the boards by two-hundred-pound bruisers was not as much fun. Over the course of the season, it became abundantly clear to me that my skill set was different than theirs.

Near the end of the season, we were in the dressing room discussing our final exams. Most of the players did not enjoy their finals, and Wayne was lamenting how brutal his had been. I was steering clear of the conversation because I had learned that when you tell someone you loved your final exams, they look at you like you're from Planet Norbert.

Wayne noticed I was avoiding the conversation, so he looked over at me and said, "Mur, how did your exams go?"

I didn't want to lie, so I just said, "Pretty well."

"How well?" Wayne asked, smiling.

I told him I got As in all my exams.

He said, "What?! That's impossible! How about your English final?" Wayne had a particular aversion to English.

I paused, weighing how I should respond. I'd found the final pretty easy, but I thought better of saying it like that. "Umm, I got a hundred percent," I admitted sheepishly.

He started cracking up. "A *what* percent?" he shot back.

I stared at the locker room floor. The entire room had fallen silent. "A hundred percent," I repeated.

Everyone roared in disbelief, and Wayne jumped to his feet.

"*Nobody* gets a hundred percent on their English final!" he gasped. "What the heck are you even doing here?" Throwing his hands in the air for emphasis, he blurted, "If I got a hundred percent on my English final, *I wouldn't even play hockey!*"

I was astonished to hear this coming from someone who loved hockey more than life itself.

My safe haven in Toronto was the family I billeted with, the Badalis. Gus, the patriarch, lived and breathed hockey, and was an aspiring scout and agent. He befriended my brothers when they lived in Toronto, inviting them to the Badali home for traditional Italian pasta feasts prepared by the matriarch, Pearl. Marty and Mark raved about Pearl's cooking and the warmth of the entire family.

If the name Badali sounds familiar, it's because just about every hockey fan has heard it. My teammate Wayne asked me what I thought of Gus, and I told him straight up he was a great guy. Honest, hardworking, and in it for the right reasons. Total devotion to the game and his players. So Wayne went with Gus as his agent.

Gus and Pearl treated me like family, and I also became fast friends with all four boys: Mike, Frank, Paul, and Shawn. The elder three and I set up a pro-worthy weight-lifting gym in the basement to toughen us up. We were all benching twice our body weight by year's end. I taught the little guy, Shawn, who was then only five, how to shoot billiards. He was so small he played by kneeling on top of the table, but he routinely beat any guests who took him up on the offer of a "friendly game of pool."

The word "tough" can mean a lot of different things. When we think of tough guys, we usually imagine people who intimidate other guys. But being around my dad taught me that it's something subtly different. Being tough doesn't mean you intimidate someone else. It means you don't let anything intimidate *you*.

My father was impressed not by the swaggerers and showboats but by the people who meant what they said and stood up for what they believed. One of those individuals was the late, great Bill Gadsby, one of my dad's closest friends. Uncle Bill was inducted into the Hockey Hall of Fame in 1970, after retiring as the highest-scoring defenseman in the game. My dad had played with him and against him, but in 1969, he was playing *for* him.

The Red Wings owner, Bruce Norris, had a phone installed at the home bench so he could call to offer "strategic advice" from his private box throughout the game. He would demand that Bill bench one player or another, and like any employee who serves at the whim of a capricious boss, Bill knew he didn't have much choice. One night, Norris told him to sit Dean Prentice. The thing was, Prentice was playing brilliantly at the time. He was also a former teammate of Bill's and one of his closest friends.

Uncle Bill yanked the phone right off the wall and pitched it. The trainer blanched as he watched Bill defy his boss, and Bill figured he'd just got himself fired. By season's end, he figured right. He didn't regret it. To Bill, integrity was more important than job security. That's true toughness.

There are a thousand examples of my father's toughness, but the story that comes to mind now involves something I'm not sure my dad would even have thought of as all that remarkable.

Dad lost three teeth early in his first NHL game. Later that same game he scored his first NHL goal. As a kid, I was genuinely curious: Is that what an NHL goal is worth? Would I sacrifice three teeth to score in the big leagues? So I asked Dad if he thought it was a fair trade. His answer? "Hell, yes!"

In other words, if you were going to try to dissuade Gordie Howe from going hard to the net, you'd better threaten to do something a lot worse than knock out three teeth.

Keep in mind that if you're playing in the NHL, you're tough. Even the finesse players, whom some fans think of as soft, are anything but. They play through injury like everyone else, plus they have to put up with the nonstop cheap shots and trash talk. The toughest guy on the roster is not necessarily the enforcer. I tip my hat to the veteran star playing on a bad knee, with his wrist taped up, getting a shot of painkiller to freeze his herniated disk.

I have a ton of respect for high-scoring players like Wayne Gretzky, who carried the weight of his team and the game of hockey on his shoulders for his entire career. Wayne was always a target, and despite being built more like a tennis star than an NHL player, he absorbed some punishing hits over his unfathomable career.

When I played junior hockey with Wayne, we once traveled to Stratford, Ontario, to face off for the semifinals of the Southern Ontario championship. Everyone's heard of Stratford because of its Shakespearean plays, medieval charm, and walking tours of fine chocolatiers. It's also the hometown of Justin Bieber. But what you may not know is that Stratford's team that year was composed of twenty of the hungriest, angriest badasses ever assembled. Even badder than Bieber.

We did have the Gretzky factor in our favor, but not even Wayne could stop this band of outlaws. We also faced a raucous hometown crowd—and apparently some hometown refs—rooting for our demise. The game was not a pretty sight. Our opponents hit everything that moved or breathed.

Our coach put out Gretzky's line to kill a penalty because when Wayne had the puck on his stick, he could hold on to it long enough to run down the clock. Sure enough, he won the face-off and skated back into our own end. He then carried the puck the length of the ice, juked the goalie out of his jockstrap, then flipped the puck into the upper corner of the net. It was one of the most brilliant short-handed goals I'd ever witnessed.

Our bench erupted in celebration. We suddenly believed that we could actually win this thing. Gretzky raised his stick triumphantly to signify a goal and circled behind the opposing team's net. Then from nowhere, a Stratford defenseman skated up behind Wayne and slammed him in the back of the head. The guy hit him so hard that it knocked Gretzky right off his feet. He landed face-first on the ice, out cold. The rink went silent, and you could feel the life drain out of our bench. Our coaches went berserk, demanding justice from the refs; they suspended the player for one game—which was a joke because this was the last game of the season.

Anyone who's ever doubted Wayne's toughness needs to know what happened next. After he woke up and was helped over to our bench, he told the coach he was ready to go back out there. The coach was astute enough to keep him on the bench. But anyone who asks to be put back in after he's had his bell rung like that in a hopeless game is a lot tougher than me.

———

I had an early peek at the world of sports medicine at the age of five, before the field was even invented. I will never forget it. I was allowed in the Red Wings dressing room after a game. I wandered wide-eyed around the locker room, trying to stay out of the way of the huge, scary-looking, toothless guys who walked naked from shower to whirlpool to ice-bath to training room.

I can still smell the Ben-Gay that permeated the room, and taste the salt tablets and glucose pills that looked so enticing until I tried a handful and then looked for a place to spit them out. I can still hear the drone of the whirlpool tubs buffeting against players bruised body parts. I stared in awe at the weary warriors who sat submerged in tubs of ice, trying to numb their battered legs and arms. I gawked as trainer Lefty Wilson, a stogie hanging precariously out one side of his mouth, stitched up a player's shin on one table, while Doc Finley poked a huge needle into my dad's elbow. The needle was attached to a syringe filled with viscous fluid, which I now realize was probably cortisone and novocaine. Dad was once asked who had the hardest shot in the NHL. Mr. Hockey replied, "Doc Finley!" These players were as tough as they came. It seemed funny to me that the team's management felt it necessary to post a sign overhead saying, "We supply everything but guts!" I mean, did these guys really need a reminder? I've never known a gutsier group than pro hockey players.

Dad introduced me to each player and made sure no one trampled me. He grabbed me a can of pop, a puck, and several rolls of tape. Dad was a scavenger, a survival skill born from his Depression-era boyhood. The Wings may have underpaid Dad for twenty-five years, but he more than made up for it in purloined locker room paraphernalia. How much would a roll of legit hockey tape pilfered from the Red Wings dressing room by Gordie Howe himself be worth now? Too bad we used it all up in our driveway hockey games.

My dad then sent me to tell Mom he would be out as quickly as he could. It would still take some time for him to get dressed. All the bruises and welts he'd sustained in the game had him moving a bit slower, but he never complained.

Only now do I appreciate how remarkably rugged he was. I had no idea back then that Dad hobbled a bit after each game because as a rookie he had torn the cartilage in both knees and had the shredded menisci completely yanked out. He played thirty-two years of pro hockey with no knee cartilage. Without those rubbery gaskets to cushion and stabilize the knee, athletes typically retire within a few years as arthritis begins grinding the bones into a jumbled mess.

Mr. Hockey's wrists were another medical phenomenon. He had fractured the navicular bone on both sides sometime early in his career. This bone has a tenuous blood supply, and if the fracture isn't recognized promptly, the bone dies and collapses, destabilizing the wrist. The arthritis in my dad's wrists was so debilitating that he had to have surgery in 1971 to remove bone fragments just so the wrist could move. The doctors told him it would take at least a year, if ever, to regain use of the joint, so he was forced to retire. As the world knows, though, he was back in 1973. He played another seven seasons with those wrists, even though they were perpetually swollen to twice their normal size. His biggest challenge was finding a watchband that could fit. Nine inches around.

In the end, I had more in common with those doctors I saw in the dressing room than I did with those bruised, battered players I admired so much. Of course, having your chin stitched up without lidocaine isn't the only way to be tough. Standing by your principles, sticking up for the little' guy, forgiving those who have wronged you, no matter how much you are hurting—that's toughness. People who are joyful, content, and loving also seem to have an uncommon inner toughness. They are not easily detoured from the things they know are important. They don't choose the easy route. They take the *right* route.

I don't claim to be tough by any stretch of the imagination, especially not on the ice. The differences between my dad and me on the ice were diametric. He dominated pro hockey for thirty-two years. I was chosen the most improved player almost every year of my amateur career. (That's not an award you want to win twice.) Dad crushed lobster claws with his fingers. I needed Vise-Grips to open up a bottle of pop. Dad enjoyed a good scrap. I avoided fights like the plague.

Dad refused to wear a helmet and wanted to wear as little equipment as possible. "Too much bulk," he said. His shoulder pads were glorified cardboard. I welcomed the shelter of a helmet with a full-face shield, bulky shoulder pads, and elbow pads the size of pillows.

I was knocked out just once, in a hockey game when I was fourteen, after I made the mistake of barelling down the ice with my head down. I woke up on the ice momentarily to see my coaches standing over me. All I could hear was the deafening gong of a huge bell. Then I was out again until I woke up an hour later in the hospital. I don't care to relive that experience. Dad, on the other hand, got knocked out so many times that he stopped counting.

I've seen tough, and I don't put myself in that category. But having been around toughness is one of the things that has inspired me. Just getting up for 5:00 a.m. practices on outdoor rinks in the dead of winter was an exercise in toughness for me. Studying all weekend for an organic chem exam felt like a cakewalk compared to skating wind sprints for two hours during hockey school. In fact, after training for most of my childhood to be a pro hockey player, I found it easy to work a thirty-six hour shift with only a few hours' sleep while on the surgery service during medical school.

Despite our differences, I've inherited a few trinkets of Dad's mettle. I've never called in sick during my twenty-six-year radiology career. That's probably an American College of Radiology record. And I don't feel normal unless my day includes something physically exhausting, like running, lifting weights, or shoveling snow. I learned from Dad to consider every chore a way to get in shape while doing something good.

In my quest to be like Dad, I also learned to persevere against all odds. I learned to never give up, to train as hard as possible, and to give everything I had in whatever I did. And to never, ever complain. Ever, never, ever. Dad inspired me—and countless others as well—to be the best people we could be. He just made you want to be better. Just as often, however, Dad seemed to be inspired by the courage and toughness of others. One shining example of that was Dad's buddy Chuck Robertson.

Chuck was one of Dad's closest friends. They were so close, in fact, that when my family moved to Houston so Dad, Mark, and Marty could play with the Aeros, I stayed behind and lived with the Robertsons. We all agreed that if I wanted to play pro hockey, it would be best for me to remain in Detroit. I ended up living with them for three years. Chuck loved me like his own son, and he never accepted a penny for room and board. I never met a kinder, gentler man. I could not have admired him more.

He was also a big, physical guy. He loved the outdoors, and he dominated at pickup hockey. Chuck didn't smoke or drink, and he kept himself in good shape. On the ice, he was one of the few players without a beer belly, and he was always a force to reckon with.

But around the age of thirty-five, he noticed that his legs started to feel heavy. He thought maybe it was just old age or varicose veins, so he went in for a checkup. A few tests led to a few more tests, and soon they had a diagnosis: a rare form of muscular dystrophy. He was given only six months to live. This particular type of muscular dystrophy was inherited.

Chuck's brother, Bill, who had no symptoms up to that point, also tested positive, and died within six months as doctors predicted. But Chuck, being Chuck, wasn't going down without a fight. He read every article that he could and went to the University of Michigan to try a number of experimental treatments. Contrary to conventional wisdom, which was that MD patients should not exercise because it "used up" whatever muscle was left, Chuck was placed on a grueling workout regimen.

He lived another forty years.

He was literally the Gordie Howe of muscular dystrophy patients. Doctors were baffled at how he held his disease at bay. Still, despite the treatments, he slowly, progressively lost muscle strength, to the point where it was difficult to walk, and eventually even to talk or swallow.

But Chuck was never one to complain. He viewed every day as a gift, and he was determined to make the most of it. He always had a smile on his face, no matter how much effort it required. He was a very proud man, and he wanted to be independent as long as possible. He refused to stay home and brood about all the things that he used to be able to do.

One time, he made a trip to Carl's Golfland in Bloomfield Hills to hit a small bucket of balls, which might take him several hours. There was a tiny step at the entrance, but Chuck didn't see it. When he stepped down, there was nothing but air, and he keeled forward, careening into a huge display of golf balls stacked to the ceiling. As he crashed to the ground, the entire pyramid collapsed on top of him, burying him. The store manager rushed to his aid, uncovering his head as quickly as he could. He was concerned that Chuck was injured, but to his surprise, Chuck was laughing hysterically.

The store manager, relieved, said, "Did you want just one box, or should I ring up the entire pile?"

——

I consider my family blessed to have had another year with my father. The fact that science and medicine can provide families more quality time with those they love is truly a great gift. But I have no doubt that my father's remarkable recovery was facilitated by who he was. This was a man with unfinished business, and he wasn't going to bow out until he'd signed a few more autographs, posed for a few more pictures, and given a few more hugs.

Mr. Hockey taught me the true meaning of toughness in his last years. He never did shrink into a little old man, remaining a physical force until his very last days. Like most people in their eighties, Dad was a significant fall risk. Yet he had no interest in a walker, a cane, or (God forbid) a wheelchair. As he exited the jet in Denver to complete the first leg of our trip home after his first stem cell treatment, a wheelchair awaited him at the door of the plane. Dad just picked it up, moved it aside, and strode down the gangplank. I had to talk him into accepting a ride through the terminal by informing him we had a mile-long walk to the next gate. I'm sure part of it was pride—riding in a wheelchair must have been difficult for someone who was accustomed to being on the cover of *Sports Illustrated*. But by the end, when even this small physical gesture was beyond him, his inner toughness was undiminished. In his last year, when speaking was tough, walking was tough, and even eating became tough, Mr. Hockey was at his toughest.

Not knowing where you are when you wake up but still mustering a smile—that's tough. Stepping to the microphone to say thank you to a crowd of thousands when you know the words might be impossible to find—that's tough. Posing for photographs, offering up hugs and elbows, and giving all you have left just to raise your hand in the air—that's tough. There will never be a tougher man.

8

Stay Positive

"I never keep track of my shots that miss."

It's half past eight. I can smell coffee brewing and hear Howes of all ages converging on the kitchen, eager to see what our neighbors have prepared for breakfast this morning. I guess part of missing someone is that everything reminds you of him. Right now, the smell of bacon and eggs is another reminder of something I'll miss with Dad.

Until two weeks ago, Dad's appetite was incredible for an eighty-eight-year-old. Most mornings he had a huge bowl of oatmeal with honey, a bowl of yogurt with raspberries and blackberries, a couple sausage links, a few scrambled eggs, a pint of chocolate milk, and a doughnut or two. Even at the end, he seemed superhuman.

Most elderly patients with severe memory loss require anxiety meds or antidepressants to level out their moods. But save for a little Tylenol and Aleve to take the edge off his arthritic back, shoulders, and wrists, Dad functioned drug-free.

Though Dad was aware of his profound short-term memory deficits, it didn't dampen his sense of humor. One morning he pointed to his chin and said, "I'm numb from here on up." I was infinitely grateful that Dad not only knew who he was, but also was keenly aware of his role as Mr. Hockey. I was equally grateful that he knew who I was, and recognized most of our family and friends.

The one time when he didn't seem to know me, which happened in the last month of his life, was actually pretty funny. He was exhausted after a long outing, and I was trying to help him get ready for bed. It was way past his bedtime and he just wanted to lie down with his clothes on and plop his head down on his Red Wings pillow. I was determined to help him into his pajamas and get his teeth brushed. He wasn't buying it, though, and after I'd spent way too long trying to get his shirt over his monstrous shoulders, he sat down on his bed, stared at me intently, motioned with his index finger for me to come closer, and said, "Come here!"

At that moment, it was clear to me that I was no longer his little guy, Mur. I was some overzealous rookie who had crossed the line. I thought about the famous photo of Lou Fontinato after he tangled with Dad, his nose on the side of his face. I looked down at my dad's huge hands and decided I wasn't stepping one inch closer. "No, thank you!" I said with a smile and a chuckle.

He persisted. "Come here," he said. "I wanna show you something." I thought about my grandfather's career as a backyard brawler.

I wasn't falling for that one. "No, thank you. I'm fine right here," I replied. "Dad, I'm your son Murray. I know you're tired. I'm trying to help you get your PJs on so you're more comfortable. But if you wanna sleep in your clothes, have at it."

His face relaxed, and I could tell he recognized me again. I moved in closer, still a bit uneasy, and helped get his pajamas on. He relinquished his partial denture to me to clean. After kissing him goodnight and thanking him for being the best dad ever, as I did every night, I walked out of his room and thought, "Whew, that was a close one!"

Save for those rare moments of sheer exhaustion, Dad was the most positive, peaceful, and joyful person I've ever known. He almost always had a smile on his face and a song on his lips. He once told me, "Don't gripe about the cards you've been dealt. And don't worry about anyone else's cards. Play your cards the best you can, and be thankful you get to play."

Dad didn't fear failure, and he didn't dwell on his mistakes. He learned from them, and then erased them. Similarly, he didn't dwell on his accomplishments. When he came home from a road trip and we greeted him at the door, I could never tell by his face whether he had won or lost the games. He knew he had given it everything he had, and in his mind, the rest was up to God (with a little help from his teammates).

———

This attitude allowed him to be the consummate competitor. On the ice he was relaxed and creative, and he kept it fun. He once told me, "I never keep track of my shots that miss." I would add that he never kept track of the shots he made either. The past was what it was. He savored the present and welcomed the future with open arms. He was eager to see what opportunities the Good Lord would bring his way that day. If God came up short, Dad would make something good happen himself.

Ditto for Mom. If she got an idea, she would make it a reality. There was no stopping her. And rest assured, she got a lot of ideas. Mom lived one of the most amazing, inspirational lives of anyone I have ever known. Her list of accomplishments showed how much she'd earned the title of Mrs. Hockey. But what made my mom so special was not her accolades or her entrepreneurship, but the size of her heart.

Although she was born in the humblest of circumstances, like Dad, my mother was driven to be a champion for the underdog. She was one of the kindest, most compassionate, thoughtful, supportive, enthusiastic, fun, adventurous, welcoming, and generous people I have ever known. Although my thoughts are focussed tonight on what I learned from Dad, my mom was equally inspiring to me. She was my biggest fan, closest confidant, counselor, and catalyst of my optimism and faith in a loving God. I am forever indebted to her for loving example.

Mom was born in 1933 to a single teenage mother. My grandmother Margaret had neither the means nor the patience to raise a child on her own. But every cloud has a silver lining. Margaret sent my mom to live with Aunt Elsie, a distant relative.

Aunt Elsie had always wanted to have children, but she lost her first husband soon after they were married. After that, her father fell ill, and the years flew by while she tended to him. By the time she was thirty-eight, she had given up hope of ever having a child. And that's when baby Colleen landed on her doorstep—truly a gift from above.

Aunt Elsie's farmhouse, in the tiny village of Sandusky in Michigan's thumb, wasn't much more than flimsy wood walls with a small kitchen/family room and bedroom downstairs and a loft upstairs. Mom and Aunt Elsie slept in the loft, which had a window with no glass, just a shutter that opened in the wind. Mom and Elsie would huddle together on cold winter nights under a mound of blankets and wake up with snow blanketing their bed. The house also lacked central heating, but it did have a large wood stove to keep them warm.

Although life on the farm was tough for Mom, she was loved completely. Aunt Elsie read to her, played with her, and took her to church daily. She tucked my mom in every night, dazzling her with stories of princesses and castles and knights in shining armor. She assured Mom that God had a special plan for her someday. With this foundation, the future Mrs. Colleen Howe grew to be unstoppable.

Her motto became "Why not?" With no work experience and a home-sewn wardrobe, she applied for a job as an executive assistant to C.S. Mott, a founding member of the General Motors Corporation. Although Mott was a Michigan industrial icon, he was a down-to-earth man and very hands-on when it came to choosing his employees. He personally interviewed each one. That particular day, he sat behind a giant oak desk and glared down at this petite but confident lass, who was just sixteen years old.

"So, young lady, tell me why I should hire *you* instead of one of the thirty other capable women I have interviewed?" he queried.

The clock ticked loudly. Cars whizzed by on the street several stories below. Mr. Mott looked at his watch.

"Well," Mom offered, "I notice you have lots of file cabinets here, and they all have to be organized alphabetically. I know the alphabet backwards as well as forwards, so I'll be able to file things twice as fast as anyone else." Then she gave him her most relaxed smile, though her heart was pounding beneath her sternum.

"Let's hear it, then." Mr. Mott called her bluff.

My mom flashed her baby blues and chimed, "ZYX, WV, UTS, RQP, ONM, LKJ, IHG, FED . . . CBA!"

Mr. Mott burst out laughing. He gave her the job on the spot.

When we were kids, my mom taught each of us how to recite the alphabet backwards, just as Aunt Elsie had taught her, and this became a tradition handed down from generation to generation. To this day, I can still do it, in exactly 3.44 seconds.

Mott later went on to make a generous donation to the University of Michigan to build a state-of-the-art children's hospital in Ann Arbor. This is the hospital where Mark underwent his cartilage-sparing knee surgery in 1971, and also where I did my pediatric radiology training. Strange to think that none of this would mean anything to me if my mother hadn't been able to recite the alphabet backwards. I'd say that's a pretty good example of the difference a positive attitude can make.

Dad first spotted Mom at the Lucky Strike bowling alley and was immediately smitten by her good looks. He asked the manager to introduce them. "Murray, she was the best-looking girl I've ever seen!" he told me on several occasions. But Dad had many fine-looking girls chasing after him, and he could have taken his pick. He married Mom because her positivity equaled his own. Together they were unstoppable, and the Howe kids, along with the rest of the world, were the beneficiaries of their indomitable spirits.

On the ice, Dad never got down, never gave up, and never let the grind of the game get to him. I'll never forget the sight of him coming off the ice after a disappointing loss during the 1970 season. The Wings were struggling then, and the players walked to the dressing room with their heads down. All except Dad. He held his head high, eyes scanning the crowd for a familiar face or a little kid to poke. "Dad!" I blurted out from behind the barricade. He flashed the slightest glimpse of a smile and winked. He knew he'd given everything he had. No regrets.

That was the most important thing with Dad—doing your best. It wasn't that he didn't mind losing. No one who ever lined up against him came away thinking Mr. Hockey didn't play to win. But he believed there is no point feeling down when you've given it everything you've got and you're still beaten fair and square. You can't control the world.

For all his legendary toughness, Dad didn't play angry. That was another quality of Dad's I had always admired. Hockey back then could be wild. There were some truly great players in the WHA, but there were plenty of thugs. And the fans could be pretty wild too. They loved the fights, and management tended to give them what they wanted. In the midst of all the shaggy-haired goons and carousing fans, Dad was so poised and graceful (and slightly menacing) that he seemed to glide through the chaos as if he were playing a slightly different game.

I remember one particularly ugly playoff game in 1975 against the Cleveland Crusaders. I was beside myself. No one wants to see a bunch of thugs taking cheap shots at his father. "I hate those guys," I remember saying to him afterward. "They were really dirty."

Dad said, "They took some liberties, but it goes both ways, Mur. And without the other team, there is no game."

Never once in his career did he complain to me about an opponent. If he didn't like what an adversary did, he just took down his number and calmly returned the favor at some future point. But he never fumed or carried around any bitterness. If he had a problem, he just dealt with it.

I also never heard Dad make excuses or blame anyone else for his circumstances. In his 1978–79 season with the New England Whalers, he took a slap shot to the ankle. It hurt, but he was still able to play. He asked the equipment manager to stitch an extra layer of protection to his skate. A week later it wasn't done, and he asked again. The following week, he asked once more. The next game, the skate still bare, another slapshot found the same spot and shattered the bone. He missed more games from that fracture than any other injury in his career.

When I flew home for Christmas vacation during my freshman year at the University of Michigan, I asked him how he'd ended up in a cast. He told me the whole story, but he asked that I keep it between us. He didn't want the equipment manager to lose his job, and he figured the manager had learned his lesson.

At the end of his last season with the Whalers, I flew out to Hartford for his retirement. During the press conference, he had nothing but kind things to say about the club. After the event, he and I walked out to his car together. He turned to me and said, "You know, I think I still have a few more good years left in me."

I said, "Well, why don't you keep on playing, then?"

He said, "It's hard to score from the bench."

Dad had been very frustrated by his lack of playing time as the coaching staff favored the younger players. That strategy failed miserably. Yet Dad never criticized them publicly.

"They're in charge," he told me. "I have to respect that. But it's just not fun riding the pines, so I'm going to find something to make myself more useful."

———

This book is not about me. This is about my father. I never doubted my father's love, but now that I am a father I understand it better. And I know that it is impossible to come close to understanding a man without seeing his children through his eyes. I know I would not be remotely the person I am if it weren't for my kids, and I believe that to be true of Dad as well. His family meant more to him than any trophy.

Parents want their kids to be happy. And kids want to make their parents happy. Motivated by love, parents can end up pushing their kids mercilessly, believing they'll be happier in the end. And a kid who knows that his accomplishments make his parents happy all too often concludes that *only* his accomplishments make his parents happy. My parents' love wasn't like that at all. But who doesn't want to follow in his father's footsteps? Those footsteps seem all the more worthy when the whole world acknowledges that your father is the standard by which others can be judged. Your dad can hit a golf ball 400 yards. Your dad can hit baseballs out of Tiger Stadium. Your dad is the greatest hockey player on the planet. I wanted to make him proud. I mean, I was a Howe, and that's what Howes do. We play hockey.

Dad loved hockey more than almost anything, yet he never pressured me to play. If he had ambitions for us kids, he never voiced them. My brothers and I played because we wanted to be like him. When he attended our games, he watched quietly, softly clapping if either team scored or made a nice play. He never yelled or shouted out instructions. He let the coaches do their job.

Still, I preferred he not watch me play. I felt inadequate compared to my brother Mark, who became the youngest Olympic hockey player ever as a high school sophomore. I was in grade six at the time and Mark seemed gargantuan to me. His biceps dwarfed my head.

Though Mark was a superstar, he was a remarkably nurturing older brother. He drove me to school every day that year, offering me brotherly advice along the way, and invited me to go golfing with him whenever he went. I idolized him completely. Mark was also extremely generous, and when he returned from Sapporo, Japan, he gave me his official US Winter Olympic team hiking boots, which I wore every day until the following summer. But that wasn't enough. When he wasn't home, I used to sneak into his drawer and pull out his Olympic silver medal, which weighed a ton, and then wore it around the house, my hands lofted overhead, imagining the adulation of the fans in the Olympic arena.

As if Mark hadn't raised the bar high enough, my even bigger brother Marty was an all-American football player as a freshman and set multiple track-and-field records that same year. He also starred on the basketball team and dominated the superheavyweight wrestling division. Marty also had a beautiful singing voice, and performed in a few of the school productions. Marty was over six feet and also ridiculously good-looking, and the girls seemed to flock to him even more than they did to Mark.

On the ice, Marty was one of the toughest players I'd ever seen besides Dad. As a defenseman he punished any opponents who dared venture near his team's net. I admired Marty as much as I did Mark. I set up an entire track-and-field area in our backyard and trained for hours, trying to imitate Marty's feats in the hurdles, high jump, long jump, discus, and shot put. The more I trained, the greater respect I had for his seemingly superhuman abilities.

One of the greatest moments in my life was inspired by Marty. In grade six, on a field day for my school—on the very same high school track where Marty had set all his records—I competed in several events, failing miserably in all of them. Adding insult to injury, I let up in the last few yards of the 600-meter run, sure I had sealed up a bronze medal, only to be passed by my buddy Bill Dunn in the last nanosecond. I was so angry with myself for giving less than 100 percent that I wanted to hit myself in the head with a shovel. I would have, had it not been for the fact that I didn't have one on hand, and also I had one more event to do: the long jump.

There were at least ten guys in my grade that were jumping far beyond me when we practiced jumping during recess. I felt I had a snowball's chance in hell of winning a medal, so I figured I'd get this event over quickly and drown my sorrows in a bowl of chocolate ice cream. But I had so much anger and self-loathing boiling up inside me as I raced down the approach lane that I launched myself into oblivion at the takeoff. I landed near the far end of the pit, at 12' 9", almost two feet farther than I had ever jumped before. It was a Bob Beamon-esque performance, and no one was more surprised than me. I collected my gold medal at the awards ceremony the following day, and even now I can still can feel the elation in accomplishing something extraordinary. Extraordinary for me, anyway.

Both of my brothers were legendary in my eyes. To say that I was proud of them would be a gross understatement. Yet I didn't envy them—I just admired them and tried to emulate them. That was another great lesson I learned from Dad. He respected the finer qualities in every individual, and that inspired him to be better himself. However he never begrudged anyone else's gifts.

In contrast to my dad and brothers, I was no more than an average hockey player. I felt as if I embarrassed my dad each time I stepped on the ice. I wanted so much for people to say, "Wow, that's Gordie Howe's youngest son! Did you see that goal! He's just like the ol' man!" I wanted to do well in hockey more for him than for me.

It was a tradition in international hockey for players to exchange pins or patches from each other's hometown as a souvenir. We would form two lines facing each another, and then skated toward an opposing player to swap souvenirs, shake hands, and say whatever seemed appropriate. This was always an awkward moment. Each of us was there to take the other guy's head off. The exchanges usually went something like this: "Um, here, this is for you. Good luck." "Oh, thanks. Well, here, um, this is for you. Have a good game." But in one particular match when I was thirteen, my opponent looked at me as if he were staring at the real Gordie Howe and said, "This is for you. I sure hope you're not as good as your dad!"

I beamed with pride and said, "Don't worry, I'm not!" I wasn't kidding. (Though I did score a hat trick that game, the only one in my career.)

It was that same year that my family moved to Houston so that Mark, Marty, and Dad could play for the Aeros. My goal was to play pro hockey alongside them one day. However, I had a dilemma: Minor hockey in Houston was in its infancy. They had two rinks while Detroit had thirty-two. I was concerned that my chances of playing pro hockey might vaporize if I moved to Houston. Mom agreed, and made arrangements for me to stay in Detroit.

Dad told me she cried all the way down to Texas, wondering if she'd done the right thing. I moved in with the family of Chuck Robertson, a good friend of my parents. I loved school and got along well with my new classmates. Plus, Chuck's son Rick and I were teammates and good buddies, and the Robertson's had four really cute daughters, Lori, Sherri, Tammy, and Jody, who doted on me. So I wasn't exactly suffering. But still, I missed my family. My decision to stay in Detroit gives you a sense of what hockey meant to me. I skated every day, lifted weights, did calisthenics and wind sprints, trained in tae kwan do, and played "little hockey" with Rick on our knees in the kitchen with a tennis ball and eighteen-inch hockey sticks. I was doing everything possible to make my dream come true.

I played three more years in Detroit, culminating in a national championship with the Paddock Pools midget team when I was fifteen. That might sound great, but the truth was, I played sparingly in the championship game—the first time I sat the pines my entire life—because the coach chose to go with our top two lines. I still can feel the frustration of being a bench-warmer, willing to swap my spleen for a chance to get out on the ice.

Truth be told, that entire year was when the fun seemed to fizzle from the game. I topped out at a not-so-intimidating five-foot-six and 165 pounds. I competed against kids who were one or two years older, and each season more players seemed to tower over me. The bodychecks got heavier, and with each injury my enthusiasm deflated even more.

The following year I moved to Toronto. Scouts who had seen me play in tournaments the prior year seemed confident I could compete at the junior level, and I signed with the Seneca Nationals. I played with a fifteen-year-old Wayne Gretzky. Most of the players ranged in age from seventeen to twenty. Wayne was the best in the league; I was quite possibly the worst. But the season began on a high note. I skated on a line with Wayne, and every time I passed him the puck, he scored. Similarly, every time I was anywhere near the net, Wayne would find me with a pass and I'd have a great scoring opportunity. I had more points my first week in Toronto than at any other time in my career. I wasn't an agile skater, but if I was going in a straight line I could haul ass, and I vividly recall a preseason game where Wayne had the puck and I instinctively headed to the net. The Great One threaded a pass through a forest of lumber and found my stick blade magically. I tipped the puck into the net, and just like that we were up 1–0. It was one of the last goals I scored that year. While I celebrated with a humbly raised stick, Wayne was bubbling over with joy. He was more excited than I was.

Then the coach moved Wayne to a different line, and shortly after I trashed the ligaments in my ankle playing rugby in gym class. That injury took three months to heal, and breaking back into the lineup was an uphill battle. I can't blame my coaches for playing me sparingly, because frankly, I just sucked. Dad watched me play a few times, and he suggested that I needed to "stop pushing the panic button." I was rushing my passes and shots, he said. Trying too hard. That rarely turns out well.

The following season, my last in Toronto, I tried out again for the Nats. Although I made the club, the coaches suggested I consider playing in a lower division to get more ice time. I ended up on the Wexford Juvenile AAA team, a far cry from the Nats but hands-down the most fun I've ever had on a hockey rink. Suddenly I was the star. Playing at that level shattered my chances of getting a hockey scholarship, but I felt like I still had a chance to get onto the University of Michigan Wolverines team as a walk-on the following fall.

There were sixty walk-ons that year, and I made it down to the final five before being cut from the squad just before the preseason opener. Coach Dan Farrell posted the final roster, and sure enough, there was no Murray Howe on it. I checked a few times just to make sure.

I still remember that moment with agonizing clarity. I watched my dreams float away like a big, brown helium balloon with a sad face on it. I needed to get out of that locker room fast and go as far away as I could. I wanted to wish the guys well, but I was too emotional. My heart was pounding. I felt as if all eyes were on me. I grabbed a piece of chalk, my hand shaking as I wrote on the board, "Good luck, guys. MH."

Coach Farrell stopped me on my way out and encouraged me to play junior hockey in Metro Detroit for the season, then come back and try out again the next year. I thanked him, but I knew it was time to move on.

To be perfectly honest, I never really quit hockey. It quit me. I guess I could have pulled a "Rudy" and stuck with it for four years of college. I could have continued to train while trying to keep my head above water in my pre-med classes, hoping that when Coach Red Berenson took over the following year, he'd put me out for one shift when Michigan was up 16–1 in an exhibition game. But I'm glad I made a clean break at that point. Better to be decapitated than slowly exsanguinate from a thousand paper cuts.

As I wandered the streets of Ann Arbor pondering my future, my first thought was to call my parents. Better that they hear it from me, I reasoned, than from a reporter. When I called them, my mom just said, "Well, think of all the wonderful doors that are going to open up for you now." That was classic Colleen Howe. Dad said, "You didn't seem like you were having much fun with it lately anyway. Better to find something you enjoy."

It is difficult to describe the freedom my parents' words granted to me. Until I heard those words, part of me believed that I had to be as good as Gordie Howe to deserve their love and pride. It was their unhesitating positivity that showed me that it was me they were interested in, not my stats. Dad wasn't trying to raise another Gordie Howe. He was perfectly happy with a Murray Howe. In the end, he was as proud of my medical diploma as he was of his Stanley Cup ring.

The negative view would be that I had wasted all those years pursuing a hopeless dream. But that overlooks the value of *trying*. I would have always wondered what might have been if I hadn't pursued my dream. It also showed me that striving without true passion would never satisfy. Four years later, I joined the Hockey Docs medical school team. Thirty-nine years later, I'm still skating and loving it. Hard work is never wasted.

———

Undoubtedly, living positively empowered Dad to weather his dementia with dignity, propelled Mom to rise above her humble beginnings, and inspired me to pursue my dreams with reckless abandon. Growing up in the Howe family, I've witnessed my parents "can do" spirit open the doors to a treasure trove of unforgettable experiences. Two come to mind.

In 1972, the Osmond brothers were the hottest boy band since the Beatles. My sister, Cathy, was in love with fourteen-year-old Donny. My parents knew this, and they took Cathy and me to their concert at Cobo Hall. Every time Donny grabbed the microphone, girls around me shrieked hysterically. Several fainted. Cathy was mesmerized.

After the show we waited outside the stage door so my sister could get the brothers' autographs. But when the door opened, they headed to their waiting limo without so much as looking up. Cathy was devastated. But Dad already had a plan.

He knew there was only one place the Osmonds could be heading. The "who's who" always stayed at the Ponchartrain Hotel when they were in Detroit back then. So we cruised over to the Ponch and I followed Dad into the lobby to see what he was up to. He found a phone, and I listened in as he called the operator and asked to be patched through to the Osmonds' manager. Moments later, Dad hung up and turned to me with a grin. "We're going upstairs to meet them!"

Dad collected Cathy and Mom from the car, and we marched over to the elevators. Cathy could hardly contain herself. "Oh my god, oh my god, oh my god" was all she could say. The elevator finally opened at their floor. We stepped out, and there, standing in the hallway outside their room, were the Osmond brothers, literally in their pajamas. Every one of them was slender, with perfect teeth and perfect hair that draped perfectly over their ears.

We chatted with them for nearly an hour. One of the Osmonds, Jay, asked Dad if hockey players wore shoulder pads. Obviously hockey wasn't that big in Utah. It was actually a valid question for the uninitiated, because Dad's shoulders were so big that it didn't seem like he needed shoulder pads. Dad autographed their pajamas. Cathy was shell-shocked and barely spoke a word.

That same year, Dad invited me to golf with him at the legendary Inverrary Country Club in Fort Lauderdale, Florida. This was on Dad's bucket list, and he wanted to share the experience with me. I'm not sure why, as I was undoubtedly the worst golfer to whack a ball around that immaculate course. Mr. Hockey golfed and I whacked. About halfway through the round, Dad realized that his golf tips were not helping; I'd lost a dozen balls in lakes, woods, and subdivision streets. I was still enjoying being with him, but I guess Dad figured he needed to cheer me up.

"You know, Mur, Jackie Gleason lives somewhere on this course. Do you want to ditch this course and try to find him?"

What kid doesn't love to see an impish smile on his dad's face?

I perked up. "Sure, Dad, let's do it!" This was the first time in Dad's life that he aborted a round of golf, so I felt pretty honored that he'd do that for me. We traipsed around a number of posh estates, dragging our clubs with us, first checking for rottweilers patrolling the yards, then knocking on doors and asking, "Is this the Gleason residence?"

After about an hour of this, we happened upon a man in his garage, halfway beneath one of the several classic cars parked in there. Dad stepped inside and said, jokingly, "Jackie, can I hand you some tools?" I have no idea how my dad knew those legs belonged to Gleason, but he was right.

Gleason laughed, a bit nervously. "Sure, I can use that ratchet over there. You aren't going to steal it, are you?"

My dad then introduced himself, and the actor rolled himself out from underneath the car. "Well, I'll be damned!" he said. "Gordie Howe is in my garage!"

For the next thirty minutes they shared golf and hockey stories and spoke about their families. I didn't add much to the conversation, since I didn't really watch *The Honeymooners*, and frankly, Ralph Kramden, Minnesota Fats, and Buford Justice all intimidated the crap out of me. I answered each question with a simple "Yes sir, Mr. Gleason." Despite my apprehension, it was a magical encounter, and the most fun I've ever had on a golf course. It was one of the nicest things Dad ever did for me.

People might assume that a man like Gordie Howe, who lived such a storybook life, didn't experience any lows after reaching the pinnacle of his career. His positivity buoyed him through whatever challenges he might have faced, but one of the most powerful lessons I learned from Dad was a result of one of his greatest trials. It's a trial that we all face at some point in life: the search for our purpose.

When I was eleven years old and Dad had recently retired from the Wings, he seemed to be at a low point in his life. His own mom had passed away the previous summer in a tragic accident. He and Mom had left my grandparents to babysit us for a few days at our family cabin while my parents flew to Toronto for a weekend appearance. That night my grandmother woke up with a headache, opened the door to the stairs leading to the basement, mistaking it for the bathroom and stepped through.

My grandmother had been my father's rock and greatest inspiration. The man of such uncommon humanity, adored by so many, was largely a product of this simple, angelic woman. Dad was devastated by her death, and he blamed himself for it. I don't know if he ever forgave himself.

To make matters worse, he hated his new job in the Red Wings front office. He was not allowed to do the one thing he desired: to be helpful. The coaches didn't allow him on the ice. The executives didn't allow him in the boardrooms. Instead, he was sent off on endless trips around the country to represent the Red Wings at league functions. He wasn't given time to spend with fans. He was on the road a ton and away from his family. And when he was in Detroit, he was given absolutely nothing to do. He was going bonkers.

One rare evening when just the two of us were home together, we sat in our kitchen, munching on cereal for dinner. Dad suddenly said, "Come over here, Muzz, and sit in my lap." This was really out of character for him. He hadn't asked me to sit in his lap for several years. I was pretty spooked, but I sat in his lap and said, "What?"

He stared at me intently and asked, "Murray, do you think I'm a failure?"

My jaw dropped. And then I smiled at the pure absurdity of what he'd just asked. Here was my hero—a man who had a greater positive impact than anyone I'd ever known—asking me if he was a failure. And the fact that he was asking *me*, a little squirt who was struggling to be even 1 percent of who this man was, made the question that much more absurd.

I laughed out loud. "No way! I can't think of *anyone* who has done more than you. Not just in hockey, but also in how you make people's day just by giving them an autograph. It's so cool that you can make so many people happy just by being you!"

He was silent for a long time after that. Then he said, "Thanks, buddy."

We dove back into our cereal and never spoke of it again. I've thought about that conversation a lot over the years. Over time, it helped me realize that no amount of fame, fortune, or achievements can bring you contentment. Dad needed to know his purpose. Mark Twain once said, "The two most important days in your life are the day you are born, and the day you find out why."

I believe Dad mistakenly thought that his purpose was to be the greatest hockey player of all time, and when he hung up the blades, he'd lost his worth. Perhaps in some small way that day, I helped Dad to see that his purpose was really to be Mr. Hockey—to be a champion for goodness, compassion, and humility. To be a hero for all. And to realize that his worth, his greatness, would be measured not by his hockey achievements, but by how much of an impact he had upon others.

9

Friends and Family Are Like Gold—Treasure Them

"Never forget where you came from, or who got you there."

It's 9:00 a.m. I didn't set out to turn the night into a vigil, but that's what happened. And I'm glad I did it. It's not just that I am happy to honor my dad in whatever way I can. It's that walking alongside these memories through the night has helped me clarify who Dad really was. Although I can no longer reach out and touch him and Mom, I feel I know them more deeply than ever before.

What I see now, more clearly than ever, is how blessed I was to have had the parents I had. My sadness in losing them both is trumped by my comfort in the thought that they are now together, reunited with each other and also with their most cherished loved ones, especially my grandmother Katy. I feel my parents' spirits burning brightly, watching over our family.

Memory is a priceless treasure. Over these past hours, I have relived a thousand cherished moments. Just for a minute, I am eight again. Mom's sitting at the organ in our living room, lost in her own thoughts as she plays and sings "MacArthur Park" by Richard Harris. A hint of a tear forms at the corner of her eye as the song ends, then she turns to me and smiles. I can see it's a tear of joy. It was the first time I realized Mom wasn't just there for me. She was a real person, with feelings of her own. It's a stirring experience, coming to know someone you love more deeply.

I had to wait a little longer to see Dad cry in person. Even after losing his own mother, he kept his tears in check. But sometimes the kindness of others can open the floodgates. In 2011, Michael Bublé came to Detroit, just in time for my dad's birthday. He invited the Howe family to the concert, and seated us front and center.

In the middle of one of his songs, he literally stopped the band and said, "That's it. I just can't wait any longer! I am so excited to tell you all that we have an incredibly special guest here tonight. One of my biggest heroes, Detroit's own Mr. Hockey, Gordie Howe, is here with his family. And it just happens to be Gordie's eighty-third birthday, so please join me in singing 'Happy Birthday' to a true living legend!"

The spotlight found my dad, and Bublé and fifteen thousand of his Detroit fans serenaded Mr. Hockey. During the song, Michael made his way down from the stage to our seats with a huge cake illuminated with eighty-three candles.

Later in the show, Michael dedicated the song "Georgia" to my mom. Then he looked down into the audience and asked, "Remember, Gordie?" Years before, he had performed at an event for my parents, and my mom had loved that song. The loss of my mom in 2009 was still fresh in my dad's mind, and the floodgates burst. Mr. Hockey was gushing—the tears never seemed to end. To see Dad's longing for Mom, this still-burly man crying his eyes out in front of thousands over the loss of his forever love, showed me a side of my father I'd never seen.

One of the traits I admired most in him was his undying devotion and loyalty to our family, especially Mom. The way he opened doors for my mom, stood up whenever she entered a room, helped her with her coat, and constantly asked her if there was anything he could do for her . . . well, I could not have had a better role model for how to be a husband. Even when Mom got angry with Dad, he wouldn't retaliate. He'd stand his ground, but discuss the issue calmly. If they couldn't reach a truce, then one of them would remove themselves from the situation to allow emotions to normalize. But they always came back.

One of the worst fights I ever witnessed was up at our cabin around 1971. My mom saw a photo from a charity golf tournament my dad had attended (no wives or girlfriends were invited), and in the photo several twenty-something "hotties" were sitting on the laps of the men. My mom referred to such women as "bimbos." No brains—just butts and boobs. Seemingly no regard for the sanctity of marriage or family.

I'd never seen my mom so incensed. She banged pots around like a madwoman, and I was afraid she was going to smack my dad on the head with one of them. For his part, Dad remained calm, acknowledged his faux pas, and tried to explain. He was just trying to be a good sport and raise some money for charity, and he wasn't a proponent of this time-honored good ol' boys tradition. But to Mom he was guilty for not taking a stand.

"I don't have to go to these tournaments if you'd rather I didn't," he offered.

"You need to go. These are worthwhile charities, and the kids are counting on you." She paused. "But from now on, I'm going too, along with any other wives or girlfriends who want to come along!"

Truce! Together, over the next few years, they dismantled the "bimbo tradition" once and for all.

Dad kept a photo of Mom in his wallet until the day he died. He looked at it every day, sometimes holding it up for me to see. It was a photo of her in her bathing suit that he took on their honeymoon. He'd stare at it for a long time, smile, and say, "Beautiful." No tears. Just gratitude.

Dad's devotion to his children was equally inspiring. Like Mom, Dad made it a point to carve out some time with each of his kids to make us feel special. Dad never did anything alone if he thought his kids would enjoy it. Whether it was fishing, golfing, chopping wood, digging a trench, or tearing down a wall, he'd always invite one of us to help him. He had a lot of time for us because he rarely watched TV, didn't spend much time on the phone, didn't go to bars with his buddies. What that meant was that he was there for us. I got tucked in almost every night as a child. Both of my parents would take a few moments to tell me a story or just listen to me. Those are some of my most treasured memories.

Dad and Marty could both fish until sunrise. One of Marty's favorite childhood memories, similar to mine, was being dropped off in a floatplane for seven days on an unnamed Northern Ontario lake—just Marty, Dad, the fish, and the bears. No phones, TV, radio, heat, or running water. They ate what they caught, and they caught lots. Marty said there were times when they were both quiet for hours, reveling in the idyllic scenery and burgeoning fishing net. He remembers that the dark woods, the bears, and the other wild creatures seemed scary, but as long as Dad was nearby, he felt safe.

Marty loved his alone time with Dad. Mark lived for it. Mark idolized Dad and loved everything he loved, especially hockey. Mark skipped school in a heartbeat to go anywhere Dad went, and he has some pretty priceless father–son memories as a result. Mark got to accompany Dad to the Red Wings training camp in Port Huron—not even my mom was allowed to go! Dad also drafted Mark as his golf sidekick as soon as he was old enough to swing a club. Either of them could have been a pro golfer. Dad taught Mark a lot about life, courtesy, and etiquette in between sinking thirty-foot putts and driving three-hundred-yard tee-offs to within a club's length of the pin.

Of course, Dad had a soft spot for Cathy, his only daughter. I remember her as a preschooler latched round his neck and holding on for dear life, like a baby rhesus monkey, while they watched a TV program together. Dad let her hang there for the entire program. Cathy's favorite memory was walking the beach at Siesta Key, just the two of them, looking for seashells. He'd find one and immediately hand it to her. Dad always wanted to spoil her. He knew he had to work harder at bonding with her because she didn't play hockey.

Dad also valued his friendships dearly, and his definition of a friend was considerably broader than most people's. He considered every fan a friend. He routinely treated strangers with more warmth than some treat their own family members. Dad had a remarkable capacity to care.

I think that care for others came from a genuine, heartfelt sense that we are all equal. We're all entitled to the same warmth and concern from others, and it is a debt we all owe to the world. His heart was big enough to care for everyone, and caring only made it bigger. I saw this first-hand, and I saw too how concern for others only enriches your life.

Joe and Gladys Reske were neighbors of ours in Lathrup. Tragically, Gladys contracted polio in 1957 while pregnant with their son John. John was born almost completely blind and deaf. The Reskes were told there was no hope for a normal life and advised to institutionalize him. They decided to keep him home, and give him all the love they had. Miraculously, John responded. He could hear, though sounds were muffled. He could see, though images were faint. Eventually he was enrolled in a school for the deaf, and flourished.

Joe brought John with him everywhere. This included visits to the Howes. Joe was a landscape architect, and would come by when there was work to be done. John was a *huge* Red Wings fan, and Mr. Hockey lived up to his reputation. Whenever the Reskes stopped by, Dad stopped whatever he was doing. I'd watch as Dad would lumber over to John, clamp his vice-grip hands around John's neck, lift him high in the air, then turn him upside down and dangle him, lightly brushing John's head on the grass. This was his way of saying "hello." Eventually he'd drop Johnny onto his head, ever-so-delicately, and then ease his size-11 penny loafer onto Johnny's chest. Mr. Hockey applied just enough pressure to tickle John's rib cage until he laughed uncontrollably and cried "Uncle!"

That was years ago, of course. John has grown up and moved away. He is married, and can see remarkably well now thanks to advances in optics. That shows you what parents' love can do even in what looks like a tough situation. My brothers and I have kept in touch with John. A few years ago, he underwent a cochlear implant, which changed his life in ways he'd never imagined. I was fortunate to be the first person to speak to John by telephone after his surgery. It was magical. He described to me how fascinating he found the sound of peeling an orange. It had never occurred to him that the peel would make a sound. A whole new world had been opened up to him, and hearing the world afresh through John's ears made everything sound new to me as well. Every time I peel any fruit, I think of John. He's helped me to appreciate the world—see things more clearly—all because Dad took the time to care.

———

I hadn't been back to Dad's hometown since my grandmother's funeral when I was ten years old. Dad had been back many times, of course. He never forgot where he came from. But Dad was also very busy. Hockey players worked in the summers back then, even the greatest hockey player on the planet. And when he did get to Saskatoon, his time was mostly taken up with fundraisers and promotional events. He talked about his family all the time, but in all those years, he'd never had a chance to sit down with them and catch up. It was one of his greatest regrets.

I wanted to remedy Dad's angst. Plus, I was dying to see where he'd played hockey as a boy, where he'd gone to school, and where'd he lived. I also wanted to see this magical "Waskesiu" place that he talked so much about. (I figured I should include some fishing on the trip. No one loved to fish more than Mr. Hockey.)

So in the summer of 2011, I organized a trip for Dad, and my son Gordie, to visit Mr. Hockey's roots. Dad was so eager to see his family that we didn't even check into our hotel when we got to Saskatoon. We drove straight from the airport to the home of my aunt Helen, my dad's youngest sister. His other surviving sister, Vi, was there, and so was Uncle Neil, who had been married to Dad's sister Joanie. From the moment we stepped out of the car, it was unforgettable.

Helen and Neil met us halfway up the walk. In front of this small, unassuming house in a small Canadian prairie town, Gordie Howe embraced his sister like any big brother wrapping his arms around a sister he hadn't seen in far too long. There were tears all around. Her little white Yorkies yapped and leapt into the air, but no one took any notice besides me. I was struck by the fact that while the world had changed around Helen and Dad, some things hadn't changed at all since the thirties. Her big brother was back in town.

Vi was waiting inside. She was in her late eighties (although she looked twenty years younger) and had more difficulty getting around, so she was content to allow her little brother to make his way to her. Vi was more reserved, and you could sense Mr. Hockey's reverence for his older sister. It was clear that she could still whoop his arse if he got out of line. She was kind, but she didn't mince words. She gave me the lowdown on my dad's childhood shenanigans.

I was blown away by how much Helen reminded me of my grandmother. Sweet and thoughtful, funny and optimistic, but most of all, devoted to her family and grateful for everything she had. She was a treasure-trove of Gordie Howe stories. One that stuck with me was when she and my mom took my dad's first-ever brand-new car out for a joyride. Helen didn't have her license, but my mom said, "That's okay, I'll teach you!" Helen proceeded to crash the car. The car was still drivable, but Helen dreaded what my dad would say when he saw the huge dent. She needn't have worried. When they arrived home, all he said to her was "You silly girl!" For Dad, people were always more important than things.

The one person missing most from the table during our visit was Grandma Katy. It's funny how being a parent changes your view of your own parents and grandparents. You begin to understand how much you mean to them. I thought about what it had to have been like for Grandma Katy raising Dad, her super-athletically gifted son, the sweet one with a learning disorder. She did it right. She showered him with love and instilled in him a sense of responsibility to do the right thing. She left the world with quite a gift.

Grandma Katy once told my sister a story illustrating both Dad's deep devotion to her and his capacity for mischief. As a young teen, he had landed a job at a Saskatoon hotel. While leaving the hotel one day, he noticed a nice plate tossed out in the trash. He asked his boss about it and was told it was chipped. Dad inspected it and concluded that it was in better shape than anything the Howes owned, so he took it home. Then, mysteriously, new plates and bowls began making their way into Mrs. Howe's cupboard, each one with a remarkably similar chip on one edge, until her cupboard was full.

I say my grandmother was missing from the gathering, but Helen found a way to bring her near. She shared a recording the family had made for my dad back in the late forties, shortly after he had left home. They had been sitting around the kitchen table. You can hear a dog barking in the background as family members lean in to wish Dad well and tell him how much they missed him. Hearing my grandmother's voice, recorded when she was younger than I am now, brought home to me forcefully just how close we are to previous generations. As much as we love our parents and grandparents, it's easy to forget they once went through all the ups and downs that we do. So it gave me chills to hear a young Grandma Katy lean into the microphone and send my dad her love. "Take care of yourself," she said. "And don't let nobody step on you."

—

Neil and Helen led us on a tour of Mr. Hockey's childhood the next day. It's an amazing thing, how the world goes on without us. It's humbling to realize that we come and go, but the world around us stays pretty much the same. Life went on in Saskatoon after Dad left, just as it would for anyone else. The South Saskatchewan River kept flowing, even though Gordie Howe had stopped skating on it, and the Grand Trunk Bridge still stretched across it, even though Dad no longer climbed along its girders to plummet a good sixty feet to the water in the summers. It's where he played most of his hockey, just a kid with skates several sizes too big and a stick he'd begged from the local senior team. This unassuming place, an old rusty bridge, is where history had happened, though it showed no sign of it.

I guess that's another thing family gives: memories that mean something only to us. It can make a rusty old bridge into something monumental.

The same is true for all the houses Dad lived in as a kid. All but one are still standing. The Howes were renters when Dad was young, so they moved a lot. As soon as the rent went up, Grandpa Ab packed up the team and headed out—sometimes just down the street or right next door. They lived at 411 Avenue L North, 413 Avenue L North, and 633 Avenue L South. This last home was a bow and arrow's shot from my dad's school, King George. So one myth took a hit that day: legend had it that Gordie Howe skated ten miles to school each day, braving the bitter prairie winds. Now I knew he lived just down the street. (There's no doubt in my mind that he skated ten miles a day, however, to and from the river, and during the course of his many games.)

We also visited 409 Idylwyld Drive, aka Avenue A, which was the house my dad bought for his parents once he'd turned pro. It's a very modest bungalow on a busy street with a little hedge by the sidewalk. Next door is a Chinese church. My dad and my grandfather worked together to install indoor plumbing—it was the family's first. Kind of gives you an idea of how different life was, not so long ago.

One of the completely unanticipated blessings in visiting all these homes was that Mr. Hockey was determined to get inside them all to see what they looked like. Every home-owner received the once-in-a-lifetime knock on the door from Gordie Howe. At every house someone was home, and their expressions upon opening the door ranged between shock and awe.

"Oh, my GOD! You're him! You're . . . oh, my GOD." They'd turn around and shout, "Ian, Wayne, come here! I want you to meet someone! It's Gordie Howe! At our door!"

My dad just smiled shyly. "Mind if I come in and have a look around? I used to live here."

Who would even imagine saying no?

"Sure, Gordie, come on in. Do you want something to drink? Are you hungry?"

We spent about half an hour at each home, eating cookies, and hearing more anecdotes of what had transpired there so long ago. Dad posed for pictures with everyone. And of course, my dad signed walls, pictures, photo albums, anything he was asked. One homeowner had compiled a history of the home and asked my dad to sign it, right on the page that talked about the Howe family.

But the person who was most amazed was Mr. Hockey. Imagine stepping away from your house as a young boy, only to return decades later, after so much had changed. And yet, there's the kitchen where your mum made your oatmeal, and over there was the ice box where you snuck the meat out of your little sister's sandwiches. Dad saw a lifetime pass with each house he walked into.

The same was true of his school. When we got to King George, I immediately recognized the old cement steps at the entrance from a famous photo of Dad standing in the center of the back row, a head above the other kids. They are all wearing KGAC jerseys and standing on concrete with their skates on.

Even though he was eighty-three, Dad bounded up those stairs. At the main entrance we were thrilled to discover that the school was open because a maintenance crew was readying it for a centennial celebration. Dad posed for photos and elbowed the crew, who gladly invited us in to look around. We stepped into the building and I was in awe.

Anyone who walks into this building will be struck by a sudden sense of the person my dad was years before. The shy farm boy who struggled to read, but just wanted to be helpful, and to make his parents proud. Could he ever even have imagined his magnificent future?

On the second floor we encountered a cool lithograph of my dad, depicting his evolution from his early years in Saskatoon to superstardom. I suggested he sign one of the dry-erase boards, and he enthusiastically obliged. He drew a giant heart and then signed his name, along with "Sorry I missed you." I wished we could have stayed to see the faces of the students and parents who visited the school for the centennial festivities.

I love imagining my dad as a student of King George. I will always think of him as the greatest hockey player (and the best father) in the world. It's mind-blowing, however, imagining him as an over-sized kid wedged into one of the little chairs, hoping that the teacher didn't call on him before the final bell. The kid who stared at the clock willing it to move faster so that he could get his skates back on quicker. To his teachers, he was just one of the countless students who passed through King George over the years. And that's how he saw himself: no one special. Just a boy who dreamed of playing in the NHL, like every other boy in Saskatoon.

The only spot we couldn't really visit on our trip back to S'toon was Grandpa Ab's original homestead shack in the town of Floral. That home vanished long ago, and the town itself has disappeared as well. One of the most famous towns in all of Canada—alongside Parry Sound and Brantford, Ontario—doesn't exist anymore, except in hockey fans' imaginations. But that doesn't really matter. It will always be known as the birthplace of Gordie Howe.

—

That evening we headed over to the home of cousin Lorrie (Vi's daughter) and her husband, Matt, for a family reunion. They graciously hosted about twenty Howe relatives, and we feasted on a superb Saskatchewan steak until we could barely stand up. It was such a rare treat for my dad to kick back and relax in the company of his Saskatoon family.

I loved listening to Dad talk about fishing in Waskesiu Lake and on the South Saskatchewan River with people who knew exactly what he was talking about. They'd been there. They knew the best spots to fish, the best lures to use, and what it was like when the weather took a turn for the worse. These people weren't just family—they were Saskatooners.

I also got a kick out of hearing my cousins calling Dad "Uncle Gordie." It never occurred to me that he had so many nieces and nephews, and each one with a story worth telling. To name a few, my sixty-year-old cousin, Brian, still competes as an accomplished sprinter in his age group—with an artificial hip. My other cousin Dave is a talented drummer in a Led Zeppelin tribute band. My cousin Janet rides a Harley and runs the local parrot rescue organization.

What floored me the most about Saskatoon was not only the unbridled friendliness of the people, but also its arts, culture, and glorious blue skies. Saskatoon is sunny most days of the year, making the cold winter temperatures much more bearable. There are also thousands of beautiful lakes, endless rivers, and rolling terrain reminiscent of Northern Michigan. Saskatoon is truly a gem.

The following morning we revved up the Ford Explorer and began our drive to the mythical Waskesiu. Mythical to my family, at least. All my life, I had heard stories about this paradise in Northern Saskatchewan. All I knew was that it's a town within Prince Albert National Park, which lies about an hour's drive north of the city of Prince Albert. It's a rustic little resort, as quaint as quaint can be, with tent cabins, log homes, a general store, and multiple ice cream shops. Perfect. The town is on Waskesiu Lake, which is pristine and full of big northern pike with gaping, snaggle-toothed jaws that bite anything that plops in the water. You might not want to skinny-dip.

It is maybe a two-hour trip from Saskatoon to Waskesiu, if you drive like a crazed American, which I do. I was amazed to see a sign for "La Ronge, 244 km" while we were on the way to Waskesiu. Dad often talked about fishing at Lac La Ronge, but I had always imagined it being on the far side of the North Pole and accessible by only seaplane or dogsled. Turns out you can actually drive there.

I'm sure Waskesiu must have seemed much farther away when Dad was younger and people travelled less. From his stories, I could tell that he thought of it as distant. But maybe that was just an expression of longing for the place. The more we want to be somewhere, the farther away it seems. In any case, the moment we rolled into Waskesiu, my dad's eyes opened wide.

Mr. Hockey immediately began pointing things out.

"That is where Johnny Bower's burger joint was. I used to go in there and help him finish up so we could get out on the golf course sooner."

Then he pointed across the main road along the lakeshore and said with a smile, "That's where your mom and I stayed. In one of those tent cabins over there. They look a little different now, but I know the location. We were right there."

Once we were out of the car, Mr. Hockey said, "Let's go down to the dock," and off he went, not waiting to see if we were coming. We walked out to the end of a long pier. "They used to have a diving board here," he announced to no one in particular, lost in the immediacy of the memory. "This is where Bill and I went for a nice swim!" He broke out laughing, remembering that the water was thirty-three degrees Farenheit that late spring day, when he dove in, pretended the water was warm, and invited the uninitiated Bill Gadsby to join him. Uncle Bill nearly had a heart attack the moment he plunged into the icy lake. "Gordie, you sonofabitch!" was all Bill could say after he caught his breath.

It was later summer when we were there, so the water had warmed up to maybe seventy-ish degrees. That qualifies as a Canadian hot tub.

I said, "Let's go for a dip!"

My dad looked at me like I had lost my mind. He may have been right, but I still thought we should go for a swim. We walked along the dock back toward shore, and Mr. Hockey toyed with a few little kids who were fishing. He grabbed the butt-end of one boy's fishing rod so the kid thought that a fish was biting his line. When he finally figured out what was going on, he turned around to look at my dad, who was pointing to my son, Gordie, as if to say, "He did it, not me!"

Another little boy looked like he hadn't caught a fish ever, and did not believe he was ever going to catch one either. He was sitting on the edge of the dock with his feet dangling over the side. One arm cradled his rod, the other was bent, elbow rooted into his thigh and head glued to his hand.

"Catch anything yet?" Mr. Hockey asked the little guy.

"Nope," the boy sighed, too deflated to even look at the person addressing him. My dad gave him a few pointers, including the best time to fish, the best bait to use based on what kind of fish you want to catch, how far out to cast, how quickly to reel, and how to get the fish on the dock without losing it. If you wanted to talk fishing, Mr. Hockey could do that all day long. I would like to tell you that when my dad cast the boy's line into the lake to show him how it's done, he immediately hooked a forty-pound pike, but that wasn't the case.

It was more like a thirty-six-pounder.

Just kidding. We weren't going to stand around waiting to see if this kid was going to catch a fish. The boy obviously was cursed, and it was best to distance ourselves from him as quickly as possible.

We walked along the beach and found the nearest bathroom to change into our swim gear. Dad donned a chocolate-colored suit, with legs openings as big as my waist. It fit him perfectly.

I led the charge into the water. I had learned from spending most of my childhood summers in frigid Michigan lakes that the trick is to dive in immediately. As soon as your head submerges, your body undergoes an adaptive, physiologic process that renders you impervious to the cold. This process is called "shock." I was surprised to find, however, that Waskesiu Lake was no colder than the water of our cottage lake in Michigan.

"Dad, it's great! C'mon in! Piece of cake!" I coaxed Dad into the water. It was still at his knees, and he was shivering. Gordie my son was behind him, but he blindly heeded my call and waded past him, then dove deep. He came up with a smile.

"It's not too bad, Pee Paw!" Young Gordie reported back to my dad. "Pee Paw" is the nickname that all the grandkids used for Mr. Hockey. Travis, my brother Mark's eldest son, started it when he was a baby. Good job, Travis. Even my siblings and I use this nickname on occasion, without really thinking about how it sounds to people around us in a grocery store.

Mr. Hockey may have been cold, but he wasn't going to disappoint his grandson. He waded out a bit farther, and then made a perfect dolphin dive, coming back up to the surface with a smile on his blue lips. We floated around for several minutes, then decided to return to the beach to dry off. But we didn't get far.

A young woman was edging toward my dad.

"Excuse me, sir, but would you by chance be Gordie Howe?"

Dad smiled sheepishly and pointed to my son. "That's Gordie Howe over there."

Gordie the Younger laughed and halted the ruse in its tracks. "Yes, I am Gordie Howe, but he's *the* Gordie Howe!"

The girl lit up with excitement. "Oh, my God! Wait right here. My husband has got to meet you. He's going to die!"

"I don't want him to die!" shouted Mr. Hockey as she bounded out of the water,

She came back a moment later with her husband and two young kids. The kids were squinting in the Saskatchewan sun reflecting off the lake, trying to get a look at this giant of a man who could make their dad act like a puppy.

"Oh, Mr. Howe, it's such an honor to meet you! My grandfather used to tell me how great you were. There's nobody like you, eh? My grandfather says you used to knock guys out with your elbow, like, every game? And then score a hat trick! Wow! I can't believe I'm standing here with you!"

"What do you mean your *grandfather*? How old do you think I am?" Mr. Hockey replied with a chuckle. "He was probably talking about my father. I'm not *that* old!"

This banter went on for a few minutes, followed by smartphone photos in every mathematically possible configuration of family members with Gordie Howe. A few minutes later we were making our way back to the beach. Mr. Hockey got almost all the way out of the lake before another family of about eight spotted him and surrounded him. The bigger the mob grew, the more certain people became that the elderly muscle-man was who they thought he was. It really was Gordie Howe. The more people he spoke with, the more seemed to be drawn to him. Soon there were a good fifty people waiting for a chance to meet this living legend. As always, he didn't disappoint. Beachgoers marveled at the huge shoulders, arms, thighs, calves, and back on this shirtless eighty-three-year-old who had dared the chilly lake.

Many of the fans asked my dad about legends of him coming up to Waskesiu back in the fifties with my mom and the Gadsbys, winning the Waskesiu pro-am golf championship in 1954, and hanging out with Johnny Bower. All true, my dad confirmed.

After Dad had spent about an hour holding court on the beach, I announced to the crowd that he needed some lunch before he passed out (actually, I needed some lunch), so we got changed and hiked across the grassy town square to a burger joint connected to an ice cream parlor. The moment we stepped in the door, my dad was transfixed. "This was it!" he announced. "This is where I took your mom for ice cream every day! We usually sat right over there!"

We ordered our food, and sat in my mom and dad's "special spot." Several of the beach fans had followed us to the restaurant, so business was booming that afternoon. Every few minutes, someone would come over for a picture, an autograph, or a handshake.

Three Saskatchewanian peewee hockey players by the names of Ty, Jake, and Travis recognized Mr. Hockey, even though he had retired decades before they were born. That always amazes me. His popularity just seemed to grow with time. I shot a group photo while my dad elbowed, strangled, and bodychecked them into hockey-fan nirvana.

Eventually we finished our burgers and made our way back out into the sunshine with our ice cream. The sun was glittering on the lake, and the scent of warm pine needles marked this as the perfect summer day.

We meandered over to an old-school tent cabin, which was now a display to show visitors what the campers used to stay in "back in the day."

My dad raced over to it. "This! This was what our family stayed in when I came up here as a kid. A big black bear stuck its nose in that screened doorway, and my mom gave it a good whack with the broom. It took off like a batouttahell!"

He ran his huge hand along the fabric doorway and stepped inside. It was a basic wooden floor with fabric sidewalls and roof. I tried to imagine how his family had all packed into one of these. Then he turned to me with a sheepish grin. "Your mom and I had this kind of cabin too. Wasn't a whole lot of privacy, as you can imagine." Then he winked at me and added, "But we didn't care!"

At that point, it was time to hit the links. The Lobstick is one of the oldest, most gorgeous golf courses in Western Canada. Mr. Hockey came alive the moment he saw the first hole. He began describing to us, in painstaking detail, exactly where he would hit his first shot and which side of the green was best to place the ball for an easy putt.

He knew this course like the back of his hand because he'd worked as a greenskeeper here for several summers—*after* he joined the Wings. He would finish his work by noon and then have the rest of the day to golf, fish, and golf some more. He actually won the Waskesiu Lobstick Pro-Am Golf Tournament in 1954. At the largest match-play tournament in North America, he outplayed the pros.

In exchange for a few photos and autographs, the guys in the pro shop let us use a complimentary golf cart to tour the course. An older gentleman recognized my dad and slowly ambled over to us. "You know," he told me, "your dad was the only man ever in this tournament to drive the back of the green on the first tee. That's nearly four hundred yards uphill—and with a three wood!" He stared at my dad as if he were looking at Zeus. "Who'da ever thought that this afternoon, I would be standing here with the great Gordie Howe himself, eh?" My dad signed the old-timer's golf cap.

Then I suggested we check out a wooded trail I had spotted just off the beach. The view of the lake on our left along the trail was fantastic, and we were enamored by all the beautiful cabins to our right, where vacationers were firing up grills and campfires in preparation for steaks and burgers. At almost every cabin someone recognized my dad, sometimes from quite a distance away. I was astonished that he was that recognizable. They dropped their spatulas and ran into their cabins to sound the alarm, then came back out and sprinted toward us as if we owed them money.

One family invited us onto their charming wooded deck for a quick drink; they were as gracious as gracious could be, and then the matriarch confided that she was the professor at the University of Saskatchewan who had bestowed my father with his honorary doctorate in June 2010. It took me twenty years of schooling to acquire my doctorate. It took my dad one hour.

We kept walking until a swarm of black flies that bit like piranhas consumed us. Darkness was descending, so we decided to catch a quick bite to eat at the same place where we'd had lunch and then pack it up for the drive back to Saskatoon. One hundred autographs and a few more burgers later, we were on our way back to the city.

———

Dad had been away from Saskatoon for nearly an entire lifetime. So much in the world had changed. But he never did. Perhaps this is the most important lesson he taught me. He could have viewed his return to Saskatchewan as a victory lap, but that was the furthest thing from his mind.

His return could have been a victory lap. When he left Saskatoon, Dad was was pretty much indistinguishable from uncountable young Canadian men over the years, something common enough to be a stereotype. He was just one more strapping small-town kid looking to make it in the big league.

In the end, he succeeded more completely than anyone ever has, and likely ever will. This unremarkable kid went on to play in 23 NHL All-Star games (even the greatest scorer of them all, Wayne Gretzky, made the All-Star roster twenty times). He was in the top five scoring leaders for 20 consecutive seasons. No one, not even the greatest of the greats, has even come close. Dad scored over 100 points in the NHL *as a 40-year-old*. He won the Cup and the league MVP awards at the age of forty-five. His final game came at age fifty-two, when he was a grandfather. He had not missed a single game that season. He was truly the superstars' superstar.

Dad would be a big fish in any pond, never mind Saskatoon. Never mind Waskesiu. But he never saw himself as a big fish, and he never judged a pond by how big it was. His outlook and actions point to a profound love of life, and a deep sense of community. Humanity. He shunned luxury, glamor, and excess, because frankly he was happy with what he had. He much preferred a campfire or a backyard barbeque to life in the fast lane. To him, nothing beat ice cream on a hot day, or a glorious sleep in a tent-cabin by the beach.

His love for life was fueled by people around him. Dad never needed to rub shoulders with celebrities to convince himself that he'd made it. He loved people enough that it simply didn't matter to him whether you were rich or poor, famous or anonymous. Everyone was someone to him. He treated the cashier at the grocery store with the same openness with which he treated movie stars and fellow pro athletes. That is sincere love for his fellow man.

Sometimes we praise celebrities for refusing to "forget where they came from." Maybe some of them do. Maybe the bright lights of fame convince people they've always been stars. Maybe that willingness to leave one's friends and family and hometown behind hints at some emptiness inside, or a suspicion that there might be something better, someone more interesting, just over the horizon. I wouldn't know. What I know is that Dad never suffered that kind of restlessness. He would never forget Saskatoon, or more precisely, the people of Saskatoon. Their genuine, generous nature made him who he was. It was there that he learned that wherever he found himself was where he should be at that time, and whomever he was with was the most important person in the world at that moment.

Imagine how joyous life must be when you look at the world like that. Saskatoon has all the charm of Paris, and Waskesiu is every bit as beautiful as the beaches of Kauai. Sisters and cousins and even fans who politely ask for an autograph are every bit as engaging as movie stars. For Dad, "forgetting" he was from Saskatoon would be like forgetting his last name. When he's back with his family, he's just one more Howe, laughing and loving life like the rest of us. He wasn't happy because he was the greatest hockey player in the world. He was happy because he loved the world greatly.

EPILOGUE

Friday, June 10, everything stood still. Time seemed to float out there somewhere, not willing to tick off the next second on the clock. My father had just passed away, and nothing else seemed to matter. TV stations had broadcast the news around the globe. The radio stations scrapped their regular programming and cleared the airways for callers to share their Gordie Howe stories. My grief, and my family's grief, was personal, but it was shared by the world.

My smartphone blew up. Hundreds of calls, emails, text messages, Facebook messages, posts, and Viber messages from family and friends. I wanted to respond to all these messages, but most of them would have to wait. There were too many urgent matters to attend to, including finalizing the funeral arrangements; writing the obituary, as well as the programs for the private and public visitations and the funeral service; and orchestrating travel plans for family and friends coming in from out of town. There is little time to yield to grief when there is so much to be done.

Fortunately—through the efforts of Colleen, my siblings and their families, our friends, the Red Wings, the Detroit police, the Ansberg Funeral Home, Father JJ, and the staff at the Cathedral of the Most Blessed Sacrament—all the parts came together. My family bonded around the kitchen table on Friday evening, choosing photos and quotes to use in the programs. We knew that these programs would be cherished keepsakes for friends and fans, so we wanted to do it right.

We chose to host a private visitation on Sunday for the Howe family and those we considered to be family—the Gretzkys, Gadsbys, Gatts, Ilitches, Toigos, Saips, Robertsons, and Badalis, to name a few. We wanted those closest to Dad to have a little more time to say goodbye. It was a long, beautiful day. What struck me most was that no one seemed to want to leave. We all wanted to be around Dad a little longer while we still could.

We left only because we had a flock to feed at home and needed some rest before the next morning. That night flew past, and in no time we were on our way to meet up with Father JJ Mech at the home of my nephew Travis and his wife, Kristine, to hash out the details of the funeral. The entire Howe clan converged around 2:00 p.m. for what was supposed to be a one- to two-hour meeting. Four hours later, we were still camped around the dining room table, four generations of family members three rows deep, including Aunt Edna. The stories just kept coming. I felt closer with my family that day than ever before. Everyone wore their love for Dad on their sleeves.

I felt God's hand at work in bringing the perfect clergyman to us at the perfect time to undertake the daunting task of doing justice to the memory of such an incomparable hero. JJ was the "little brother" of our longtime friend Kathleen Winn, who was our daughter, Meaghan's, godmother. Father JJ had presided over Meaghan and Doug's wedding the previous summer, and he had really impressed us with his dignity and warmth. Dad had attended Meaghan's wedding, stealing a dance with her at the reception before retiring for the evening. It was one of the greatest moments of my life.

———

Tuesday morning came too soon. The Howe family arrived at Joe Louis Arena at the crack of dawn so that my brothers and I could serve as pallbearers for the beginning of the public visitation.

Before we rolled Dad out on the ice for the final time, family and friends congregated in the corridor where the Zamboni was parked. Only three months earlier, we had stood in the same spot before Dad stepped out into the spotlight to blow out his eighty-eight candles in front of a standing-room-only crowd at the Joe.

As we waited, Walter Gretzky regaled us with story after story of Dad. He and Wayne shared one memory of the awards banquet when Wayne, then ten, first met Dad. The banquet's master of ceremonies asked Wayne to say a few words, forgetting he was just a boy. Mr. Hockey reflexively grabbed the microphone and said, "Anyone who scores 378 goals in a season doesn't need to say another word."

Wayne, Scotty Bowman, Red Wings GM Ken Holland, and Detroit Tigers Hall of Famer Al Kaline joined my brothers and Dad's buddy Felix Gatt as pallbearers. I was ill-prepared for the overwhelming scene that awaited us. Joe Louis had been transformed into a shrine to Mr. Hockey. A spotlight shone on Dad's retired jersey banner and the four Stanley Cup banners flanking it in the darkened arena. A central red carpet was bordered by two enormous white number 9s projected onto the floor; a table of priceless memorabilia and dual screens displaying hundreds of extraordinary photos were at the front.

We guided Mr. Hockey's casket to its resting place, front and center, just about where the slot would be in front of the net. Dad's favorite spot on the ice. At 9:00 a.m., friends and fans were invited to proceed down the red carpet toward Dad to pay their respects, view the photos and memorabilia, and then, on the way out, share their stories at a station the Red Wings had set up in front of the Gordie Howe statue. The footage was later assembled into a touching video called "9 to 9: Gordie Howe Fan Memories." I was struck by the fact that all these people shared the love that I felt for my father.

None of this should have surprised me, but it did. I was stunned. Those waiting to say goodbye to Mr. Hockey stretched the entire length of the arena, then wound themselves like a mile-long python through the concourse level, out the exit doors, and around the building. I was told that fans had slept outside all night to make sure they'd have a chance to get inside.

We had planned to keep the doors open from 9:00 a.m. to 9:00 p.m. Our family was so concerned that we would have to turn fans away—and Dad never turned anyone away—that we decided to split the aisle into two lines, doubling the number of people who could move through at once. Even doing this, we kept both lines open until after 10:00 p.m., making sure that all who wanted to pay their respects could do so.

Originally we'd envisioned a few of us taking turns greeting visitors at the front of the line while the rest of the family stood off to one side, available if fans wanted to say hello. But the sincerity with which fans shared their memories of Dad compelled me to greet everyone. I could not turn away. Stories of a fan whose dying wish was to be buried in a Gordie Howe jersey. Stories of people who named their children after Dad. Stories of people who were inspired to care for an ailing spouse just as we'd cared for Dad. Stories of people who had overcome injuries and adversity to achieve their dreams. The stories never ended.

I shook hands or hugged over half of the fifteen thousand or so fans who walked up to Dad's casket to say their goodbyes. Many became choked up as they began telling me what my dad had meant to them. Then all of us became choked up. Many brought gifts and symbols of their devotion—full-size portraits, oil on canvas, framed photographs. One artist had carved an intricate Gordie Howe totem pole–style walking stick. Many of these mementos must have taken days to create. Had they stayed up all night, every night, since his death?

I cried and laughed along with everyone else. At first only my siblings and I were greeting the mourners, but as I listened to these moving testimonials, I wanted everyone in the family to hear. I grabbed my Saskatchewan-tough aunts, Helen and Vi, and brought them over to meet some of Dad's fans. When I introduced them as "Mr. Hockey's big and little sisters," you could imagine what a thrill it was for people to realize that these women had known Gordie Howe the boy, had watched him walk around the house in his skates, and had witnessed his metamorphosis from shy prairie boy to hockey legend.

Colleen, Meaghan, Doug, Corey, and Davis joined in, along with all the other nieces and nephews. It was a rare opportunity for visitors to meet Dad's beloved extended family and share their love for this man. I spoke with several people about their experience getting there that day. Some had travelled from overseas. Others had driven all night from Quebec, Ottawa, or the Maritimes. No one complained about the drive or the long wait in line. Colleen's cousin Tom Connors voiced the unmistakable feeling of commonality, of gratefulness at having known Gordie Howe, and of the huge sense of loss at his passing. No one wanted the goodbye to end. Tom lingered in the pedestrian tunnel to the parking structure, swapping Gordie Howe stories with a stranger for over an hour.

It was after 11:00 by the time we started the hour's ride home. I realized then that we'd been going for the better part of sixteen hours. My feet were sore, but my heart was soaring. I was on cloud nine, reliving all the stories I'd just heard. There were several that I decided to incorporate into the eulogy. I'd managed to condense my words into thirty minutes of pure, unadulterated Mr. Hockey—but not the twenty minutes Father JJ had suggested. I decided I would bend the truth and tell him I'd pared it down, and then talk a little faster than normal on game day. I figured I could always go to visit the confessional afterward.

———

We woke up on Wednesday morning to a beautiful sunrise. After a light breakfast, we began the trip back to Detroit. I felt the weight of the funeral—and a final goodbye to Dad—looming as we made our way into the Motor City.

When we arrived at the cathedral, an hour before the 11:00 a.m. service, I was struck by the throngs of people already waiting outside. Many represented media outlets (the entire service was to be broadcast live across Canada), but many more were a mixture of loyal fans and hockey greats alike. It seemed that not only were all of our family and close friends there, but so were many members of hockey royalty, including league commissioner Gary Bettman, the entire Ilitch family, Bobby Orr, the Hulls, Wayne and Janet Gretzky, Yvan Cournoyer, Detroit coach Jeff Blashill, Steve Yzerman, Joey Kocur, Kris Draper, Pavel Datsyuk, Henrik Zetterberg, and countless more current and former Red Wings players. I greeted as many of the nine hundred or so attendees as I could.

I found my place alongside Colleen and took a brief moment to pray for the Holy Spirit to speak through me, to make every story, every point meaningful to the audience, and to give me the words that would do justice to this legend, my hero. The older I've gotten, the more I try to give my challenges up to the Good Lord, relying upon Him to do what I can't. It's a lot healthier than worrying, and I've found that God can accomplish a helluva lot more than I can.

Dad had never led the league in church attendance. When he was in grade three, a crusty Sunday school teacher told him to read a scripture passage before the entire congregation. He said "I can't," meaning "I haven't learned to read." She heard "I can't," meaning "I don't want to." She forced him to stand at the lectern, struggling to sound out the first word in the passage for what seemed an eternity. A few snickers arose from the crowd. Dad's spirit was crushed, and he sprinted out of that church, never to return. Only in his golden years did he learn to separate the baby from the bathwater. I was amazed that a man who had undergone such a traumatic experience had so faithfully embraced the Golden Rule. I learned from Dad that the Good Lord's spirit will find you, wherever you are, in His own way, and that a beautiful faith is one that is lived more than one that is preached. (A fan once asked if he was saved, and Dad just laughed and said, "I was so bad, Jesus had to save me twice!")

Soon the service commenced, and I was invited to the lectern. I was not nervous. I was not fearful. I knew Dad was there—not in the casket but above us all, watching, smiling, and cheering me on. I had no intention of letting him down. I felt I knew him intimately, and I knew exactly what he wanted me to say.

What I found surprising as I began to speak—and it was something my brothers had both warned me about—was the audio delay. The majestic Romanesque cathedral with its vaulted archways was so immense that my words took some time to filter all the way to the back. When I said something humorous, there was not an immediate chuckle. Instead, a slow, subtle wave of laughter traveled rearward.

The chuckles ignited in the front pews to my left, with my old friend Craig MacFarlane, the renowned blind athlete, in the first pew with Wayne and Janet Gretzky, and Dad's bodyguards immediately behind them. The wave then rippled over our closest friends and family, with my wife, my siblings, and my children front and center. And finally it gained momentum, rolling over the Ilitches and on to the who's who of the hockey world, interspersed with more friends and fans. How incredible to be able to pay tribute to my father in the presence of my entire family and closest friends, along with most of our extended Red Wings and NHL family, Detroit mayor Mike Duggan, and Michigan governor Rick Snyder, all at one time.

I paused for the chuckle wave to crash against the stained glass at the rear before continuing. I was pleased at the laughter, and even the tears, that my words seemed to evoke from the crowd. I felt like everyone could feel Mom and Dad in our midst, and I am confident that they both felt so much love that day.

After the eulogy, Father JJ delivered an awe-inspiring homily. He led us all to a question: What was Mr. Hockey's purpose?

In that moment I recognized that what made my father special was not that he was different from the rest of us. It was that, as much as we all admired him, and as incomparable as his legacy has turned out to be, we are all like him in an important way.

The singular theme that resonated throughout the service was that while Dad was a great hockey player, he was an even better person. Better because he so unselfishly shared himself with everyone. Beloved, because he belonged to each and every one of us.

Dad's greatness emerged from unyielding conviction, courage, and confidence in his talents; a welcoming, forgiving, nonjudgmental heart; a fortitude to reach beyond himself for the common good. Most importantly, he used his gifts for others, and shrugged off any suggestion of his own greatness.

I think people adored my dad not because of his stats or his awards, but because they sensed that he was not fundamentally different from them. He inspired them, because they saw that they could be like him, in much the same way that I saw that. We can't all be the best hockey player in the world, but we can all be great people.

Even as we gathered to contemplate my Mr. Hockey's life, it occurred to me that there are many unsung heroes among us, or in the making, with inspiring stories waiting to be told. We all possess the ability to accomplish something extraordinary—something uncommon and inspiring—through how we live. Perhaps Dad just stood out more because he could fire a wicked wrist shot off the crossbar with one arm.

—

June 19, 2016. Nine days after Dad passed away, I awoke to a brilliant, sunny Father's Day morning. Rays of sunshine found their way through slits in our bedroom curtains. I had slept for twelve hours, my first chance to get a full night's sleep after the three-week roller-coaster that led up to Mr. Hockey's passing.

But I felt good. No, more than good—I felt great. Granted, I had just said goodbye to my father, my most cherished role model, supporter, protector, friend, and inspiration. But I knew that Dad wasn't really gone. He had just vaulted one level up, to a better view, and had left all his aches and pains behind. I also knew that Dad had lived one of the most inspiring lives I've ever known, and he'd done it with dignity, right up to his last breath. Lastly, I knew that we as a family, with the help of thousands upon thousands of loyal friends around the globe, had just given him a champion's send-off. During the 2016 Stanley Cup finals, Gordie Howe billboards and banners plastered the streets of downtown Detroit. The number 9 lit up the entire side of the Blue Cross Blue Shield of Michigan building. Radio stations opened the airways for days of call-ins so that fans could share their own Gordie Howe stories. TV stations ran tributes, and

NHL broadcasts featured game-time commemorations at the arenas; commentators took time during intermission to share their favorite Gordie stories. The newspapers carried full-page spreads honoring Dad, some with moving narratives and op-eds, while others simply displayed the number 9 across the page. Everyone in Hockeytown understood.

As I lay there in my bed, contemplating the funeral service and all the events of the previous days, I lamented that I could not hug my father on this Father's Day. Grief, however, was not in my wheelhouse. Mom and Dad were my role models, and they always seemed to be way too positive to grieve openly themselves, even though they were quick to comfort grieving friends and loved ones. From them, I learned to channel loss into something positive.

Then it hit me. There was something I could give my dad for Father' Day. What finer gift could a son give to a father than to put down in print forever the things he had learned from him? Although he wasn't a philosopher or a biblical scholar, Mr. Hockey possessed an uncommon Western Canadian wisdom. He instinctively lived life to its fullest, never wasting a moment on fear, anger, or regret. *Carpe diem*, as the Roman poet Horace so eloquently put it. *Carpe diem* indeed.

Ultimately, this would be a book about lessons learned from an uncommonly good person. My goal would be to pay tribute to my wonderful father, and also to share his perspective of what's truly important. To paint an even more intimate por-trait of Gordie Howe, the humble servant and loving dad, and his impact on me, his happy-go-lucky son, "the little guy." To tell stories of his heroism and humor, and my experiences growing up with Gordie Howe as a mentor, coach, and teacher, doing his best to keep me from embarrassing myself too much. (God knows Mom couldn't do it all alone.)

I wanted to give wings to Mr. Hockey's beautiful spirit. In fact, I felt compelled to do this because the global reaction to Dad's passing had made it clear to me that Gordie Howe fans still wanted to feel that connection with their hero.

I shot off an email to Nick Garrison at Penguin Random House Canada, who had published Dad's latest book, *Mr. Hockey: My Story.* I described what I wanted to do. He liked the idea and suggested the framework of nine lessons passed on to me from my extraordinary father. I realized I had already done that as I kept my vigil writing the eulogy. I had already relived all those memories that revealed to me the ways in which I wanted to be like him, and all the ways in which he had shown me how.

ACKNOWLEDGMENTS

This book is dedicated to:

The Good Lord, to whom I owe everything.

My parents. I am so grateful to have known you.

Colleen, my bride, for your unconditional love, and your invaluable editorial input and guidance. You are, and will always be, my joy and inspiration.

Marty, Mark, and Cathy, for your generosity, unwavering love, and for taking the time to share so many priceless anecdotes and insights into our phenomenal parents. I could not have written this book without you.

Meaghan, Doug, Gordie, Kaity, Corey, Davis, and Sean, my greatest treasures.

Our wonderful extended Howe family, for their unending kindness, including Aunt Helen, Aunt Vi, and the entire Saskatoon Howe clan.

—

More than anything, I hope this book has captured a life. I hope it's not just a list of accomplishments, but a glimpse of the richness that can be lived every day. Dad would be the first to tell you that you don't accomplish any of the important things alone. And in any case, the people he would want to thank are the same ones I have come to know and respect and admire over the years. Thanks for everything you've given our family.

Thank you to:

Nick Garrison, associate publisher at Penguin Random House Canada, for believing in me, and for sharing your world-class editorial guidance.

Marty Connors for your invaluable literary insights and encouragement.

Dr. Nancy Fordham, Lynda Schmitz, Aunt Edna, and Felix Gatt for your friendship and proofreading talents.

The Moore clan, for welcoming me into your wonderful family so completely.

The Badali, Omer, and Robertson families, for adopting me as your own.

The amazing Parkinson family, for adopting Corey as your own, and for reintroducing us to the beauty of Saskatoon.

Mike Myer, Harold St. John, Mike Mankowski, Nick Parillo, and the Tam-O-Shanter staff for making the rink Dad's second home.

Thanks, too, to all our friends and neighbors at Bear Lake.

The students and faculty of the Juilliard School of Dance, Toledo School for the Arts, the Toledo Ballet, and Company C Dance Studio for supporting Sean, and for teaching the Howe family the incalculable value of the arts.

My brilliant friends and partners in Toledo Radiological Associates, for your dedication to our patients and the community, for inspiring me to be the best I can be, for fostering an environment that allows me to pursue all of my passions, and for the privilege of being able to practice in such a rewarding field for so many years.

Promedica Health System leadership and staff, from CEO Randy Oostra to the clerical staff and technologists who work so hard to provide each patient with the best experience possible. Thank you for all you do.

Our irreplaceable friends and neighbors in Sylvania, most especially Sandy Yobbagy, who never let a day pass without delivering a hug to Mr. Hockey.

Dad's bodyguards, Lionel, Pedro, and John, who went above and beyond.

The Hatcher family, for showing us the meaning of sacrificial love.

I've already mentioned Dad's late, great friend Bill Gadsby and his wife, Edna (who, by coincidence, was from Saskatoon). Like my dad, Bill was from Western Canada (Calgary), played semi-pro baseball in the summer, and loved fishing and golfing. My parents befriended the Gadsbys as newlyweds while vacationing in Waskesiu in the early fifties. Mom and Edna instantly became the best of friends, and so did Dad and Bill. If there was one person my mom respected more than any other, it was Aunt Edna. She is one of those rare people who radiates so brightly she literally lights up any room. Her warmth and caring demeanor make everyone she meets feel instantly loved and appreciated. She is one of the most intelligent, insightful, thoughtful, funny, and fun women I have ever met. So deep was my parents' respect for the Gadsbys that they named them our legal guardians.

If my mom and Aunt Edna were like peas and carrots, then my dad and Uncle Bill were like sequoias and redwoods. Big and quiet, they enjoyed each other's company without saying a whole lot. It was hard for them to get a word in edgewise once Mrs. Hockey and Aunt Edna got rolling. But Dad and Uncle Bill didn't need to talk. They were perfectly happy to swing a golf club. Or cast a lure. Or deal a hand of bridge. When guys from the Canadian prairie had something weighing on their minds, the last thing they wanted to do was "share their feelings." They preferred to whack, chop, smack, or smash something really hard until they felt better. But if Mr. Hockey ever did need to confide in someone, he knew that he had an ear to bend. An exceptionally big ear. Thanks, Bill and Edna.

Thanks as well to another family who has been with the Howes through thick and thin: the Finleys (the late, great Doc Finley; his wife, Genevieve; and their cadre of five lovely daughters and son Michael, a fellow physician and my former teammate). Jack was the Red Wings team physician for most of Mr. Hockey's career, and he became very close with my dad. Due to HIPAA regulations, I am not at liberty to divulge the things they talked about over the course of my father's six-decade career, but suffice it to say that if my dad had any physical, psychological, or emotional challenges, Dr. Finley was his "go to" man.

Another physician I must thank is my mentor, Barry Gross. Dr. Gross was an extraordinary radiologist at the University of Michigan, and he inspired me to pursue diagnostic radiology after dazzling my second-year medical school class with 3D images from a CAT scan. Barry became my residency director and was a phenomenal role model as a physician. The skills I learned over the years allowed me to guide my parents' and family's healthcare needs confidently and compassionately. Barry also taught me how to keep it fun, just as Dad had always emphasized. He met Mr. Hockey on several occasions. Dr. Gross was in awe of his hockey hero, and Mr. Hockey was in awe of this man who had so inspired his son. Barry is one of the brightest, yet most modest, physicians I know.

The Ilitches also had an immeasurable impact on Dad, and the rest of the Howe clan. They have been so thoughtful and generous to our family over the years that it would be impossible to catalog all their acts of kindness. One of the humblest, yet grandest, gestures that stands out in my mind happened in 1982, just after Mike and Marian purchased the Red Wings. Right away, they brought Mr. Hockey back home to Detroit. Literally. The prior owner, Bruce Norris, had strict orders not to let Dad anywhere near the dressing room—payback, perhaps, for his signing with the WHA. But the Ilitches immediately reconstructed Dad's locker-room stall and invited him back to suit up once again. From then on, Dad knew that the Red Wings, and the Ilitches, were family. His stall remains in the locker room today, and perhaps for all time.

Mike said then, "Gordie Howe set a standard of greatness with his play that I've always tried to uphold as the owner of this storied franchise. Gordie was the greatest player of his era, and his grittiness on the ice embodied the hard-working spirit of Detroiters. I felt it was important to honor all that he has meant to this franchise and the city of Detroit." In 2006, the Ilitches constructed the Gordie Howe Entrance to Joe Louis Arena. In 2007, they unveiled the Gordie Howe statue, a bronze-and-granite behemoth towering a good ten feet over the Gordie Howe Entrance.

In September 2015, our family watched a preseason game with them from their box. The Ilitches could not have been more gracious, and they made sure everyone was well fed and taken care of. Before the game, Dad cruised through the Detroit dressing room to elbow a few players and coaches and pose for photographs. It was an unforgettable sight to see the love and respect shown to Dad by Coach Blashill, the training staff, and stars like Datsyuk, Zetterberg, Dylan Larkin, Jimmy Howard, and Drew Miller, to name a few.

It is remarkable how profoundly some people can impact your life. Randy Omer, an irrepressibly energetic, funny, and fun-loving real estate broker from Owosso, Michigan-gone-wild, was one of those people. His only speed was a million miles an hour, like a little boy who had just downed an entire shipment of Sugar Smacks. Randy led, and everyone followed. You just had to. He was having so much fun that you couldn't resist.

Dad met Randy in 1966 on a Panamanian fishing trip arranged by Al Philpott. Al invited Dad, Bill Gadsby, and my godfather, Ed Taube. Ed in turn invited Randy and Bill Doolittle, the coach of Western Michigan's Broncos football team. None of them were ever the same again. They caught a ton of marlin and sailfish, and bonded as if they had been best friends since childhood. Randy told my dad and Uncle Bill, "You guys have gotta come up to Bear Lake! That'll be a weekend you'll never forget!" He was right.

"Waddyasay, Coach!" Randy said as I hopped out of our station wagon. He put out his hand like he was going to shake mine, but the moment I put my hand out, he stepped in and gave me a big bear hug. Randy couldn't always remember names, so he called everyone "Coach." Soon he himself was known as the Coach, which was perfect because that's what he was.

Coach introduced us to his irresistably sweet wife, Susie, his sons, Robin and Lance, and his daughter, Kim. We all bonded instantly, then Randy shouted, "Hooooo-oooooe, get your suits on! It's time for some water-skiing!" That was the last time any of us stood still that weekend. Coach taught us to water-ski, dirt-bike, sail, and fish for rainbow trout using corn as bait. We were up with the sun for a "dippy-doo" in chilly water, and we peered up at the Milky Way in that same water as we skinny-dipped after sunset. Dad described the azure-blue lake as "Drinking water you can play in."

Randy taught all of us how to have more fun than we'd ever experienced, and my parents fell in love with the Omers and Bear Lake. We visited their cabin each summer for three years until my parents had saved enough money to buy their own right next door. There went the neighborhood.

Thanks, too, to Corky Matthews, for letting the Kid demolish a building with a backhoe.

In Dad's later years, another man who also profoundly affected his life was Felix Gatt. Felix was barely five feet tall. My dad often rested his elbow on Felix's head and said, "This is my half brother." But looks can be deceiving. Felix is a mountain of a man.

He and his late wife, Rita, emigrated from Malta as youths, and Felix opened a printing company in Royal Oak called

Creative Impressions. From the moment he arrived in Detroit in 1953, he was a huge Wings fan, and especially a Gordie Howe fan. He collected any memorabilia he could while hanging out at the Olympia, and also going to signings and Wings events.

Felix was so generous at charity events and auctions that he became legendary with the players and the organization. The Wings had Felix on speed dial because they knew that if they had something special to auction for a good cause, he would buy it. Felix never cared about money. He was much more concerned with supporting a good cause, and with honoring the players who sacrificed themselves for the game he loved so much.

Felix attended one of Dad's book signings around 1995. After the signing, he noticed my parents carrying loads of stuff to their van and pitched in to help. They bonded instantly, and my mom invited Felix to help out at future signings. He was thrilled, and that was the beginning of one of my parents' most enduring friendships.

Felix attended almost every appearance my dad made, doing whatever was necessary to help. He also donated his printing talents, creating thousands of Howe photographs for signings and never charging my parents a dime. For Felix, this was a labor of love.

Mr. Hockey and Mr. Memorabilia got along so well that after my mom became too ill to travel, Felix became my dad's preferred travel companion. He accompanied Dad to Los Angeles, Vancouver, Calgary, Edmonton, Winnipeg, Toronto, Boston, Miami, Houston, Alaska, and beyond. Remarkably, Felix always paid his own way, and he also wrestled with my dad for every dinner tab. In Mr. Hockey's twilight, he often stayed with the Gatts when he did signings in the Detroit area.

Meanwhile, Dad enjoyed playing with the many grandkids Kevin, Connor, Amanda, Nicole, Noah, and Mikayla, as well as David and Sarah, who lived next door. David frequently coaxed Dad outside with a soccer ball. David and Sarah's parents, Jackie and Fred, found it easier not to watch these matches where Mr. Hockey would elbow, trip, clutch, or sit on their son. David loved every bruising minute of these matches.

Rita spoiled Dad with her famous mostaccioli and apple pie. He felt right at home. But Felix's most remarkable gift to Dad, to our family, and to hockey fans everywhere, as well as a lasting tribute to his beloved wife Rita, is his astonishing collection of hockey memorabilia, which he's donated for display in the Howe Museum, slated to open fall of 2017 as an integral part of the Little Caesars Arena. This collection is the most incredible assemblage of hockey memorabilia I have ever seen. It is Felix's personal Hall of Fame, and it features Gordie Howe and more Gordie Howe (with some other cool stuff from Gretzky, Yzerman, Coffey, Lemieux, Lindros, Lidstrom, Datsyuk, Crosby, Federov, Sawchuk, Abel, Lindsay, and countless other hockey icons).

Mr. Hockey's life was also enriched by many other great friends, including the Ciccolinis of Toronto and the Badalis. And of course so many people from the Detroit Red Wings organization, including trainers, coaches, and decades of great teammates like Lindsay and Abel. And then there were the neighbors on Rymoor; the people of Sylvania, Detroit, Hartford, and Houston; every Canadian; and every hockey fan.

Thanks as well to all those who so graciously celebrated Dad's life in the months after his passing. In 2016, the Howe family was treated to a moving tribute at the Vancouver Giants game, which we witnessed from the Toigo family box, where we were graciously hosted by Ron and Michele Toigo; their youngest daughter, Rebecca; and Michael Bublé's down-to-earth father, Lewis. The highlight of that evening was watching Colleen's hair-raising spin around the ice on the Giants golf cart, driven by VP Dale Saip.

The following day, the Saskatoon Blades junior team hosted a number of events, beginning with a moving luncheon where a number of former stars, including Doug Barkley and Morris Lukowich, paid homage to their hero. Morris emphasized the impact Dad had upon him as a boy.

"In a chance meeting when I was ten years old, I met Gordie in an Eaton's store in Saskatoon. From that time on, I prayed every night to play with Gordie Howe. I worked hard to follow that dream, and was fortunate enough to be drafted by both the NHL's Pittsburgh Penguins and the WHA's Houston Aeros."

Playing in the NHL was something every Canadian boy aspires to, and Penguins GM Wren Blair asked Morris if he wanted to play in the upstart WHA or play with the Penguins in the "Big Leagues." Morris didn't hesitate. "Well that's easy, Mr. Blair, I just want to play with Gordie Howe!"

Morris continued, "It was the best decision I ever made. One of my fondest memories of playing with Gordie was sitting next to him on the bench. He turned to me, and wiped his sweaty brow off on my shoulder. I thought to myself, 'Wow, I've REALLY MADE IT TO THE BIGTIME!'"

Following the luncheon was another tear-jerker on-ice tribute, at which legendary broadcaster Bob Cole, former NHL stars Bryan Trottier and Gerry Pinder, and I had the honor of saying a few words. Earlier that day, at an interment ceremony, my family placed some of Mom's and Dad's ashes into the base of Mr. Hockey's statue at the Blades arena, as well as christened the Gordie Howe Bridge crossing the South Saskatchewan River.

In November, the Red Wings held a heartfelt tribute during one of the home games. In December, our hometown of Sylvania celebrated Dad at Tam-O-Shanter arena with a tree planting, the unveiling of a memorial plaque and boulder that welcomes visitors, and a heart-warming photo display commemorating Dad's tete-a-tetes with the young players at the rink.

My wife, Colleen, entered Tam-O-Shanter recently to show the display to David Hah, a close family friend and a big Gordie Howe fan. Afterward, David witnessed two young hockey players, about seven years old, in the parking lot locked in a heated debate. "I'm going to be the next Gordie Howe!" one proclaimed. His buddy corrected him, "No, I am!" Clearly Dad's spirit is alive and well.

Dad's spirit also lives on through a number of charitable endeavors, including the Howe Foundation, the Gordie Howe C.A.R.E.S. pro-am hockey tournament for Alzheimer's research, the Gordie Howe Initiative for traumatic brain injury, and ProMedica's Gordie Howe Center. Plans are also under way for a Gordie Howe museum to be unveiled as a part of the eagerly anticipated Detroit sports and entertainment district, and in February 2017 President Donald Trump and Prime Minister Justin Trudeau called for the "expeditious" construction of the Gordie Howe International Bridge connecting Detroit and Windsor.

The link between the two countries is something that has defined our family. And I am delighted that the link will continue for another generation. At Dad's Kinsmen tribute dinner in Saskatoon, my brother Mark handed my son Corey a tray of drinks and pushed him towards a group of young women and his destiny. Corey fell hard for a truly irresistible lass named Davis. From that point on, they have been inseparable, and my son will more than likely make his permanent home in his grandfather's beloved Saskatoon. Not in a billion years would I have imagined that one of my sons would fall for a Saskatoon girl.

But Davis is the kind of girl you wish for all your sons to marry. She is kind, funny, lovely, and smart, and she's a nurse. So nothing fazes her—not even subzero temps in May. And her family is equally amazing. Corey wrote Davis an unforgettable song to commemorate the night they met and he called it "Oh, My God, Eh." It sums up how our entire family feels about this Canadian treasure.

And finally, Dad was enriched and inspired by the many great players who came before, during, or after him, including Maurice Richard, Bobby Hull, Bobby Orr, Steve Yzerman, and of course Wayne Gretzky. And I must not forget the countless devoted fans who routinely expressed to Dad how much he meant to them. Dad was as moved by their reverence as they were by his transcendence.

One fan in particular impacted Dad in a most unlikely manner: he gave him a daughter-in-law. I met my future bride, Colleen Moore, while doing sit-ups at the University of Michigan. But I soon faced the same problem many young men had come up against over the years: Colleen's father, Gerald Moore Sr., was quite strict. He wanted the best for his lovely daughters, Kathy, Colleen, and Cheri. (Jerry also had two sons, Jerry Junior and Chuck.)

Suitors couldn't just show up anytime for a date. They had to wait at the front door and be grilled by Mr. Moore. If Jerry really liked them, he would allow them into the foyer, but no farther. That foyer rug was like the Berlin Wall. You did not even attempt to cross it. But when Colleen brought me home, Jerry invited me in, and we sat at the kitchen table and talked hockey for about an hour. Fortunately for me, my future father-in-law was a huge Gordie Howe fan.

Jerry Senior was such a big Mr. Hockey fan that when he and his wife, Maureen, were expecting a child in 1961, they vowed that if the child was a boy, they would name him Gordie. As it turned out, they had a girl, and the Moores by chance named their new daughter Colleen, the same name as my mother. Hard to argue with destiny.

I was never happier to be a Howe than that night. Mr. Moore told me that when he was stationed overseas during the Korean War, his father would write him long letters describing in "bigger than life" detail the play-by-play of the most recent Wings game, starring Gordie Howe. "Your father was unbelievable," Mr. Moore said with a gleam in his eye and a huge grin. I had to agree.

After waiting patiently for more than an hour, Colleen had finally had enough of this ESPN Classics wrap-up in her kitchen and said, "So are you going to date my dad tonight, or are we going to go out somewhere?" I got the message. The moment my parents met Colleen, they fell in love with her, just as I did.

As my parents approached their golden years, Colleen always made sure their needs were being met. She inspired me to be the best son I could be for my mom and dad. This culminated in our inviting Dad to live with us in the last year of his life, and that allowed Colleen the opportunity to shower him with love for the balance of his days. It was the best decision I ever made.